HISTORIC
FRENCHTOWN

HISTORIC FRENCHTOWN

Heart and Heritage in Tallahassee

JULIANNE HARE

Charleston   London

History
PRESS

Published by The History Press
Charleston, SC 29403
www.historypress.net

Cover image: The Renaissance Center stands as a centerpiece of Frenchtown redevelopment. The building is jointly owned by the City of Tallahassee and Leon County and features public parking, office and retail space. *Photo by J. Hare.*

First published 2006

Manufactured in the United Kingdom

ISBN-10 1.59629.149.4
ISBN-13 978.1.59629.149.2

Library of Congress Cataloging-in-Publication Data

Hare, Julianne.
    Historic Frenchtown : heart and heritage in Tallahassee / Julianne Hare.
        p. cm.
    Includes bibliographical references and index.
    ISBN-13: 978-1-59629-149-2 (alk. paper)
    ISBN-10: 1-59629-149-4 (alk. paper)
    1. Frenchtown (Tallahassee, Fla.)--History. 2. Frenchtown (Tallahassee,
Fla.)--Social conditions. 3. Frenchtown (Tallahassee, Fla.)--Ethnic
relations. 4. Tallahassee (Fla.)--History. 5. Tallahassee (Fla.)--Social
conditions. 6. Tallahassee (Fla.)--Ethnic relations. I. Title.
    F319.T14H37 2006
    975.9'88--dc22
                                    2006027169

CONTENTS

ACKNOWLEDGEMENTS

My public thanks and personal gratitude go to Althemese Barnes, executive director of the John G. Riley Center/Museum of African American History & Culture, for continuing to provide me with encouragement and friendship as I endeavor to recount the history of Leon County. Her steadfast determination to preserve the story of our past has been a continuing source of inspiration to me and an amazing gift to our state. Ms. Barnes shared her insight, considerable historical knowledge and much of her personal time to help me tell a small part of the story of one of Tallahassee's most historically significant neighborhoods.

The collective memories of a multitude of people are included in the text, and the assembly of data, photographs and images is the result of the generosity of many individuals. I am particularly indebted to Terry E. Lewis for his willingness to contribute the data and photographs he collected in Frenchtown back in 1966.

I would like to acknowledge those who took the time to share their personal memories, especially Ms. Spears; Mrs. Bessie Harden and the After Lunch Bunch at Bethel Towers Apartments; and Lucille Williams and Ann Hinson, members of Bethel Baptist Church. Others who went out of their way to help me include Joanna "Jody" Norman and N. Adam Watson who help maintain the Photographic Collection at the Florida State Archives, Patty Poppel at the Tallahassee City Attorney's office and the indispensable Leslie who works for the Tallahassee Urban League. My thanks also to Dr. Lucy Patrick and her staff at the Strozier Library at Florida State University, especially Mr. Bert Altman, who invested long hours in helping me locate valuable resources and secure electronic scans of old photographs. Lee Yawn of the Tallahassee Trust for Historic Preservation helped me unearth significant information and reporter Margie Menzell graciously provided important research materials.

Finally, I want to publicly thank my husband Tim who patiently puts up with my writer's quirks and continues to encourage my passion to preserve history for future generations.

INTRODUCTION

Tallahassee's Frenchtown community is alive with the sounds of restoration, demolition and new construction. Urban planners, city officials and Front Porch Florida transformer-types can be seen wandering about, taking notes on clipboards and scribbling down concepts of future improvements. Traffic flows up and down Macomb Street, led by cell-phone-connected commuters shortcutting their way from the campus of Florida State University to close-in, northwest Tallahassee suburbs. StarMetro buses serve the area almost daily between the hours of six and ten with both residents and students aboard. Occasionally, young men cruise back and forth, their car radios pounding with inner city versions of old slave-chant-rhythms.

Turn down a side street and you will discover all that is worthwhile in Frenchtown. Neighbors here still have front-yard barbeques, children still cross through yards to visit school chums and pets laze away the day under shady trees. There is a church on almost every block. Talk with some of the Frenchtown "old-timers"—elderly ladies fanning themselves on porches and cautious middle-aged gentlemen perching on folding chairs playing card games. If you take the time, they will tell you tales of days that passed not all that long ago. They remember what Frenchtown was like during the good times and the bad. They will retell stories told to them by mothers, fathers, aunts and uncles and add some first-person accounts of the history they made themselves. They talk about their children growing up and moving away and of all the people that influenced them along life's journey. Grandparents and old teachers are remembered fondly and with respect.

This land has known prosperous times, hard times—moments of happiness and flashes of pain. This land has felt the footsteps of warring tribes, conquistadors, Spanish settlers, French explorers, red-coated British troops and Andrew Jackson's ragtag American

From left to right: Harrel Hardwick, R.D. Martin and Charles Carney played cards in the park on a recent Fourth of July. *Photo by J. Hare.*

expansionists. This earth has suffered the loss of its sons and daughters through Indian, civil and foreign wars. It has felt the sting of a slave's tear.

Former residents were hunters, farmers, military men, tradesmen and craftsmen, Indian chiefs and ex-bondsmen. Their women—of every race and ethnic background—went about their chores, honed amazing domestic skills, gave birth to and educated generation after generation. No matter their origin, no matter their religion or gender, these people learned to communicate with one another and they shared one thing in common: a deep desire to live on a land they could have and hold as long as the birds flew and the streams flowed and no government tried to take it away.

They may have arrived here five or fifty years ago. They may have come from lands across the sea or from other places in the new United States. Maybe they never lived anywhere else. They were residents of the area we know today as Frenchtown. Their stories are beyond numbers, and the legacy they leave offers insights into all the reasons why we cling to our families, friends, neighbors and the land.

Chapter 1

LAND WITHOUT FENCES

Beneath the red clay and soft-sand soils of the north-central Florida hills lay arrowheads and scraping tools formed with precision by ancient Timucuan Indian tribes. Scattered above them are remnants of the agrarian life led by subsequent divisions of the Apalachee and Lower Creek tribes and the latter-day Seminoles. A few Indian temple mounds remain. The Timucuans were virtually annihilated when the white man came. They were slaughtered, carried away as slaves and fell victim to a laundry list of European diseases that were previously unknown in the Americas. It is estimated that close to three hundred thousand Indians died of smallpox, measles, influenza and yellow fever.

Early explorers classified the Creeks into two basic groups—each of whom had distinctive variances in language. The Upper Creeks spoke a Muskogee dialect and the Lower Creeks communicated with Mikasuki nuances. The Lower Creeks bonded with remnants of the Apalachee and eventually became known as the Seminoles. Originally, they lived in small clan-groups that were tied to larger villages for purposes of protection and governance. Woody areas and meadows alike were home to plentiful game. Deer, rabbit, bear, fox and the Florida panther roamed the land and the hunting was good. For the most part, they built their homes alongside rivers. Those, as well as nearby lakes and the Gulf of Mexico, yielded all manners of fish and seafood. The skies and marshlands offered a wide array of fowl.

In spite of the abundant wildlife, the Indian people led a largely agrarian life and were skilled in cultivating a variety of produce. They were adept at clearing trees to make room for the crops they grew. Corn, beans, several types of melons, nuts and pumpkins provided a large part of their diet. In addition, they gathered wild fruits and berries.

Longleaf pine trees once covered most of the southeastern United States, but extensive clearing and logging took a serious toll. Today, aggressive reforestation efforts are helping to bring back this important resource. *Photo courtesy of the Florida State Archives Photo Collection.*

Stickball was a favorite game of the Indians who populated the Red Hills of Florida, Georgia and Alabama. *Photo courtesy of the Florida State Archives Photo Collection.*

Geologically, this area of Florida is unlike any other in the Southern United States. Leon County is divided by an east to west feature known as the Cody Scarp. The scarp was formed thousands of years ago when sea levels were much higher. The characteristic marks an area where elevations drop from heights of 230 feet to 50 feet in a relatively short distance and where the red clay soil in the north changes abruptly to soft sand in the Woodville Karst Plains to the south. There is a high level of sinkhole activity in this zone that attracts geologists from all over the world. There can be a huge lake in evidence one day and nothing but a dry pit on another as water gets sucked into Florida's unique aquifers. The water may return in a few months or over a period of several years, but it does return. The existence of the Cody Scarp explains why so many people were drawn to the northern part of Leon County where the rich soil supported an abundance of flowers, ferns, mosses, trees of all types and almost any agricultural product you can imagine. In the beginning, we know that thousands of acres of Southern land were also thickly

covered with longleaf yellow pine. This was the land the Indians cherished and the white man coveted.

You can almost hear the echoes of those who called this place home for thousands of years. Perhaps you can hear the laughter of Native American children playing games with crudely fashioned balls. The Apalachee children—and adults—played a type of stickball that was common among many Southern tribes. The game had several versions. Its object was to hit a tall pole with a ball that was hurled with a "stick" reminiscent of those used in today's lacrosse. Competition could be fierce or largely ceremonial and often helped to hone the skills needed in battle with neighboring tribes and to gain the courage to face intruders.

There is archaeological proof (discovered in 1987 by Calvin Jones) that the explorer Hernando De Soto camped near Tallahassee the first winter of his 1539 expedition. It is easy to imagine the fear that spread among the Indians and to invoke the frightened tones of trusted sentries reporting the arrival of small ruddy-skinned men wearing coverings that shined like silver and carrying odd-looking sticks that sparked with flame

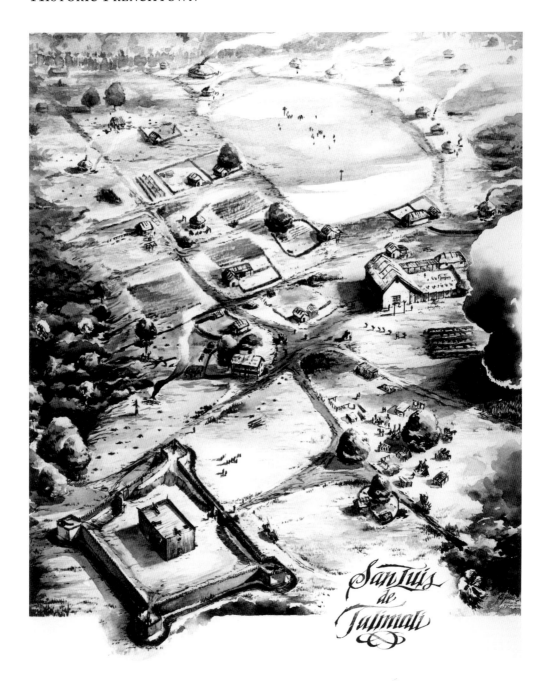

San Luis de Talimali sat at the western edge of a string of mission settlements established by the Spanish in the sixteenth and seventeenth centuries. *Original watercolor courtesy of the Florida State Archives Photo Collection.*

and smoke. De Soto's journals record numerous confrontations with some of the Indians his party met, but they were able to stay in the Tallahassee area with relative safety for a period of months. The Spaniards selected comparatively high ground to the south and east of today's Frenchtown where there would have been grassland for their 250-plus horses. De Soto's group of over six hundred men carried small trade goods and trinkets that they probably exchanged for the corn, grains, sweet potatoes and squashes cultivated by the Apalachees. It could be said that Tallahassee was one of America's first marketplaces. The visitors also supplemented their diet by hunting for game. Even today, it is easy to conjure up visions of De Soto's men tromping through the low-lying, almost marsh-like Frenchtown area to look for deer and waterfowl.

The explorers moved on, but not for long. In the ensuing years, France, Great Britain and Spain fought over the right to occupy the land known as the Floridas. The Spanish initially prevailed. They colonized St. Augustine and Pensacola. Under the direction of Franciscan priests, they built a series of over one hundred missions that stretched from St. Augustine on the Atlantic coast to deep within Florida's northern interior. Today's Tallahassee area was selected as the western "capital" of the mission trail. The priests selected a hilltop some two to three miles west of today's Frenchtown and began construction on the Mission San Luis de Apalachee in 1646. These men of faith were in the company of Spanish soldiers and a few settlers. Archaeological work at the San Luis site indicates that local Indians moved their villages to live nearby. Together, these diverse groups formed what seems to have been a vibrant community. By 1675, an estimated fourteen hundred souls resided in or near San Luis.

Perhaps it was too much to hope that possession of the Red Hills of Florida and the partnerships formed between the Indians and these new residents was enough to guarantee peace. In 1704 Governor James Moore of South Carolina led raids into north Florida. He destroyed most of the Spanish missions and Indian villages. There is historical evidence that these attackers brutally murdered priests, Spanish soldiers and settlers and captured over thirteen hundred Indians who were transported to the Carolinas, Georgia and the West Indies as slaves. After this vicious intrusion, the area around Frenchtown lay silent for many years.

Chapter 2

THE FOUNDING OF A CITY

L eon County is famous for the massive moss-decorated oaks that dot its landscape. There is an old Indian legend that recounts the time of beginning when the four winds divided the earth. The Southern Wind selected our corner of the world, and blew and blew until the grasses and flowers flourished and the trees sprung forth in great profusion. The Northern Wind—in a misguided attempt to help—draped the trees with icicles. While it was very beautiful, it did not suit the fancies and overall plan of the Southern Wind. She blew more soft breezes until the ice changed into flowing strands of vegetation. She was much pleased.

Many years later, when the Spanish claimed this land, the white man began calling it Spanish moss. It is now harvested, treated, packaged and shipped all over the country for use in floral arrangements and is a constant source of fascination to visitors. It was in part one of the reasons the Americans selected the spot they did to be the capital of their newly acquired territory back in 1824.

The land called the Floridas was fought over by many nations, but it was the Americans who were destined to possess it. Valuable farmlands along the country's eastern corridor had already been gobbled up and Americans were eager to expand their real estate. Western migration was escalating and it made little political or tactical sense to leave Florida in the hands of a foreign power. Andrew Jackson first invaded Spanish-held Florida from the west in the early 1800s. In 1821, after a series of bloody incidents and confrontations—not to mention political wrangling in Europe—the Americans prevailed. They took official possession in separate ceremonies held in West Florida's town of Pensacola and East Florida's city of St. Augustine. Initially, efforts to unite the two territories into one were made by alternating the location of organizational meetings. One year, conferences would take place in Pensacola; the next year, meetings were held in St. Augustine.

By 1822, settlers were already spreading toward middle Florida from the east and west. Near its heart lay several Indian villages called Fowltown by the whites. The Indians were living on some of the most fertile land in all of north central Florida. Two of Jackson's aides, Colonel James Gadsden and General Robert Butler, already had ambitions to own large portions of the same area. Newly appointed Territorial Governor William P. Duval was pressured to remove the Indians from their stronghold. He called for a meeting with the Indians and some seventy of them traveled to Moultrie Creek in response. The Indians were told that they were expected to "move south" and were given promises of property, livestock, farming equipment and a guarantee that their new lands would never be attacked by Americans. Most of the tribal leaders agreed to a treaty that set aside some four million acres as reservation lands. Six of the chiefs resisted the offer. Neamathla, chief of Fowltown, was among them. As an alternative to moving to the new reservation, he was "given" four square miles near the Ochlockonee River for himself and the thirty-odd families of his clan-group. Governor Duval succeeded in driving many of the Seminoles into the swamplands of central Florida but knew he would have to encourage further settlement or risk having the Indians return. Besides, alternating meetings between Pensacola and St. Augustine was already problematic.

There is an oft-told story that men were selected from each city to locate a site suitable for the new capital. As the legend goes, they were to leave their respective settlements at the same time and stop at whatever point they met. In reality, the general site was agreed upon long before John Lee Williams and Dr. Charles G. Foster departed from Pensacola and Dr. William H. Simmons and his party left St. Augustine.

Williams and Foster set out from Pensacola in an open boat in October of 1823. According to William's records, it was "steered by a boy named George," who is believed to have been of African descent. They encountered rough weather and the good doctor was tossed overboard into the waters of the Gulf. He survived, made his way to dry land and reunited with his fellow travelers. They were tested by several other trials. At one point, they ran out of food. William's journal indicates they once "lost their way," had to backtrack and find their route again. This would indicate that they clearly knew their destination.

Simmons traveled on horseback and took an overland route. Although his party had to cover rough terrain through underbrush, thick woods and swampy land, he arrived far less stressed than his counterparts. They met at a predetermined location, made their way to Neamathla's village and reportedly asked permission to build a "capital" nearby. The Indian concept of a capital would have been markedly different from the white man's. It is likely the chief envisioned a single large council house that would exist for the mutual benefit of all—not an entire city. Nonetheless, he acquiesced in some manner. Papers were drawn up, gifts were exchanged, Neamathla made his mark and the white men rode off.

The area that stretched out from the ruins of the San Luis Mission was striking in its natural beauty. In addition to the towering oaks draped with Spanish moss, the designated search party noted rolling green hills and a cascading waterfall that dropped some twenty to thirty feet into a large pool. They sent word to Duval that the hoped-for, perfect site had been secured. Gadsden and Butler were delighted.

In 1824 a group of new settlers—including John McIver, members of his family and an unnamed mulatto man—set up temporary tents and a frontier town was born. The Pringles, Blakes, Bettons, Bryds and Browns arrived in quick succession. Judge Robinson brought some of his slaves from the plantation he had already established on a tributary of the Ochlockonee River. They felled trees and hastily constructed a few crude wooden buildings. Robert Butler was named the territory's surveyor general and is alleged to have had a hand in laying out the original plat for the town. Other historians claim that honor belongs to Augustus Brevoort Woodward, who had just arrived from Michigan to assume his new role as judge of the superior court for the middle district of Florida. Whoever designed it, the town limits were set at one square mile. Provisions were made for government buildings, a cemetery, churches and several city parks. Soon the third Florida Legislative Council had a place to meet and, indeed, it was roughly halfway between Pensacola and St. Augustine. Emigrants streamed in from North and South Carolina, Georgia and East Florida; all were eager to take advantage of the "government" land being sold for $1.25 per acre. City lots varied in size and preferred location and were purchased by planters and ordinary people according to their resources. Duval was given his choice of property. He selected a small rise with a view of the beautiful cascades. Wealthy planters brought their slaves with them and amassed huge holdings in short order. Farmers with more children than livestock purchased smaller parcels of land. Tradesmen established first one business and then another, and a few African Americans who had lived freely under Spanish rule moved in.

Before long, the town had been named Tallahassee—an American version of the Indian name Tallahassa, roughly translated to mean "abandoned fields." Within a year's time, there were 120 structures and 800 residents. There were two hotels, several taverns, at least one church, a school and a brickyard. In Bertram H. Groene's *Ante-Bellum Tallahassee*, he cites an 1827 issue of the *Pensacola Gazette and West Floridian Advertiser* in which Henry Brackenridge said, "The natural open groves of hickory, beech, oak and magnolia surpass in magnificence the proudest parks of the English nobility." Changes occurred rapidly. A few years later, Comte de Castelnau, a French botanist, visited Tallahassee and observed, "The habit of carrying arms is universal. Every man has constantly on him a Bowie knife and, when he is on horseback, he has a long rifle in his hand." Resident John S. Tappan added, "You can not walk the streets without being armed to the teeth."

Chapter 3

THE NEW FLORIDIANS

Tallahassee was officially incorporated on December 9, 1825. The Florida territory's legislative council decreed that it would be governed by a mayor and a five-member city council. Dr. Charles Haire was appointed to serve as the first mayor. The small town's early residents were nothing if not an eclectic group. Men of means came with slaves in tow, hoping to make new fortunes by selling lumber to the shipping industry or by planting sugar, tobacco and cotton. Enterprising merchants and tradesmen arrived with dreams of opening new businesses and offering services in one of America's fastest growing frontiers. A few doctors, lawyers and circuit-riding preachers seized their own chances to serve this diverse group of brave souls who were willing to carve new communities out of the Florida wilderness. Included among them were military survivors of the Revolution, the War of 1812 and the First Seminole War. Politicians came to Tallahassee in the beginning and—now and forever—shall be part of its continuing history. They were joined by the likes of the disposed Crown Prince of Naples, Italy, Achille Murat, nephew of none other than the general of the French Revolution and emperor of France, Napoleon Bonaparte. Other Europeans came from Germany, Holland, Ireland, Scotland, Great Britain and other countries to escape privation, persecution or simply to start a new life. Living among them were simple farmers from as far away as Russia or as close as the east coast of Florida. Outnumbering them all were the slaves of African descent who came unwillingly and persons of color who could trace their roots back to the Indian Americans and escaped slaves who lived in relative freedom under Spanish rule.

One early resident was a black-skinned man who had been born into bondage but was living as a free man as early as 1830. Antonio "Tony" Proctor claimed to have been born in Jamaica in 1743. He was fond of telling stories about his many adventures—most of which rang true with details that he could not possibly have had knowledge of unless he had witnessed them firsthand. Antonio was "assigned" to a British officer and taken to Canada. He claimed to have been present during the assault on Quebec in 1759 and at the Battle of Lexington in 1775. Tony said he followed the redcoats throughout the Revolutionary War. At some point during Florida's British occupation, the officer and his servant made their way to St. Augustine. No one knows what happened to the officer, but Antonio claimed that by the time the United States took possession of East Florida, he was fluent in Spanish and several Native American dialects. He was pressed into service as an interpreter for the American military during the First Seminole War.

Proctor was awarded his freedom in return for his service. He also received a parcel of land in East Florida, but he sold it and moved to Tallahassee. Somewhere along his fascinating life-journey, he acquired a wife and started a family. Whether he lived off the proceeds of his land sale or earned his living some other way is uncertain, but local legend says he was called upon several times to use his interpreter's skills. In the meantime, his eldest son, George, grew and acquired quite a reputation as a builder. Some of the homes he constructed still stand. He commanded a fair wage for his skills and amassed quite a bit of money. In 1839 George purchased slave Nancy Wells for an unknown sum of cash and several notes of variable interest that reportedly totaled almost $1,300. They were married soon after. George bought land believed to be near present-day Lake Ella (north of the original city limits and east of Frenchtown) and built a beautiful home.

In 1840 sixteen free blacks were enumerated in the city. George was the only one listed as a head of household. He settled in with his father and new wife and started a family that grew by at least seven children. George was an exceptional craftsman but a poor money manager. He was deeply in debt. Sometime around 1849, he left everything behind and set off to replenish his fortune in the gold fields of California. His family did not fare well during his absence. Nancy and the children were allegedly sold back into slavery to satisfy some of the obligations he left behind. Antonio lived with his daughter-in-law for many years but died at the home of local banker Henry Rutgers in 1855. No one ever challenged his claimed age of 112. His death commanded a full obituary in the local paper. George never returned. He appears on the 1850 Federal Census taken in Sonoma, California, as a miner living in a boardinghouse. By 1860 he had returned to carpentry. He died in Sonoma on December 26, 1869.

One of the earliest and largest landowners among Tallahassee's eclectic group of residents never stepped one foot in the territory, but he may have played an important part in Frenchtown's development. In 1824, the American government awarded $200,000 in cash and his choice of a full township (thirty-six square miles) to Marie Joseph Paul Yves Roch Gilbert Du Motier, Marquis de Lafayette in gratitude for his service to the fledgling United States during the American Revolution. Lafayette had a long-standing relationship with the Butler family while in the military. Pierce Butler fought beside the Marquis during the Revolution.

This likeness of the Marquis de Lafayette was painted by Charles Wilson Peale in 1781. *Public domain image from the Images of American Political History at:* http://teachpol.tcnj.edu/amer_pol_hist.

Lafayette was so impressed by him that he presented Pierce with a sword as a token of esteem. The Marquis once said, "When I wanted a thing well done, I ordered a Butler to do it." Lafayette could have heard about the wondrous north Florida hills in correspondence or conversations with Robert Butler. Lafayette also had connections with General Gadsden and several other powerful men who had moved to Tallahassee. In any case, he selected Township 1N, Range 1E in Leon County, Florida, as part of his gift and engaged the services of several agents to handle the related legal work.

Lafayette was adamantly opposed to slavery. He believed he could establish a profitable plantation somewhere in the South through the cooperative efforts of land-lease holders and paid labor. He dreamed of transporting French settlers to America who would engage in general farming, grow silk worms for export, cultivate grapes and start spectacular New World vineyards. Correspondence between James Gadsden and F.K. Hugar of South Carolina would indicate that Lafayette and at least some of his countrymen had tried the experiment unsuccessfully in Alabama, but they were willing to attempt it again.

Legend has it that the Marquis's agents arranged for a group of fifty to sixty "Norman peasants" to settle on his new land sometime around 1831. Reportedly they built a large communal-living building on the shore of a large lake located on his grant (now named Lafayette in honor of the general). They planted groves of lime, mulberry and olive trees and set about the business of cultivating silk worms. The first year was a difficult one for these industrious farmers. A lack of adequate supplies and a series of illnesses took their toll on the little community and almost half of the original farmers died. Some headed out for New Orleans and the remainder moved into town and established a small community in a newly platted section northwest of the town's center. As the story goes, locals dubbed the subdivision Frenchtown after the home country of its primary residents.

Unfortunately, very little proof exists to support this theory of the origin of Frenchtown's name. In fact, a considerable amount of evidence can be found to disprove it. To date, no documentation has surfaced that records the French settlers' voyage to America. A group that large would most likely have landed first at a major port, such as Charleston, South Carolina. From there, they would have taken another ship to a Georgia port or to Fernandina, Florida. In either case, they would have completed their journey by an overland route. They could have sailed from a major port, then around the peninsula of Florida and on to St. Marks—just south of Tallahassee—but ships coming into St. Marks almost always carried much-needed supplies. The arrival of so many new settlers at once would have been cause for a celebration that would have been heralded in local newspapers. No such reference has been found.

Historians have located several pieces of correspondence that were exchanged between General Lafayette, his agents and others that indicate it was his intent to establish such a colony. Sharyn M.E. Thompson and Darlene P. Bowers prepared a thoroughly researched report for the Historic Tallahassee Preservation Board of

European settlers established several vineyards in Leon and nearby Jefferson Counties but not until many years after the alleged arrival of Lafayette's farmers. French-born Emile DuBois built his San Luis Vineyard near the old mission site. He is seated in the center of the front row. The others are unidentified. *Photo courtesy of the Florida State Archives Photo Collection.*

Trustees in 1987. Their work was published under the title *Historical and Architectural Survey of the Frenchtown Neighborhood, Tallahassee, Florida.* They relate sections of several such letters, including one written in 1825 by Governor Duval who encouraged the general to send some "active and industrious" people to settle in Leon County.

Robert Williams, who had verifiable Florida land holdings located in nearby Gadsden County, was known to have speculated in real estate. He would have been a likely choice as an administrator looking out for Lafayette's interests. Contents of an April 1833 letter, written by Williams as an agent for the Marquis, contained the observation, "I find our French emigrants mere adventurers without capital, improvident, and bad economists." He could have been referring to a group of settlers, but the evidence implies Williams was talking about just a few individuals. Thompson and Bowers located only three ownership agreements for parcels on the grant that appear in the names of Theodore Charles La Porte (also seen as Delaporte in some records), Isadore Gerradine and Monsieur Adams. Court records indicate there were subsequent charges filed relating to their non-payment of notes connected to the land. While it is possible that each of these men had other emigrants in their charge, none of those documents refer to any persons other than those three men.

A careful search of city documents gives us more tantalizing clues that Frenchtown was not named for the remnants of a Lafayette-sponsored colony. Early maps show this section of land as being "Reserved for the City." The area was officially designated as the Northern Addition of Tallahassee several years later. Lots of varying sizes were laid out in a box-like grid. Several persons of wealth were listed as original owners, including William Kerr, Joseph Linn, Thomas Brown, John Curruthers and the firm of Blake and Parish. All of them purchased multiple parcels, presumably for speculation, but most of them lived in other areas of town. The only buyers whose names may have been French in origin were Joseph DuPont and Benjamin Tennille.

The federal census conducted in 1830 does not indicate where residents were born. A very unscientific glance could lead a researcher to conclude that perhaps four early Tallahasseeans may have had ties back to France: Hugon, Lambert, Flotard and Clinard. By 1840 the list included Sanguinette, de Corce, Rypole, Bezeau, Fontaine, Murat and Garrardine. Historians have identified several of these individuals though other sources. Jacques Hugon arrived in Florida long before the Lafayette settlers allegedly did. He painted carriages and an occasional house and worked with wood in various ways. Lambert came in 1828. His occupation is unknown, but his son was a baker. To date, very little information has been uncovered about Flotard and Clinard, but they were not listed among the town's residents in 1840. Jean de Corce arrived in the United States in 1827, but he lived in the St. Augustine area before coming to Tallahassee. According to Thompson and Bowers, de Corce was identified in an early newspaper article as "an officer in Bonaparte's war." If so, he may have been known to Lafayette. Documents also clearly connect Garrardine to Lafayette.

By 1850—almost eighteen years after the alleged demise of the Lafayette "colony"—census data included place of birth. At that time, nine persons born in France were residing in Leon County. All of them were enumerated in Division Eight, which included Frenchtown. Jean de Corce was still in the area, but had already started calling himself by the more "American" name of John. He told the census taker he was a farmer, but at age sixty-six, there is some doubt as to how much work he was actually doing. On the other hand, a woman named Mary who was living with him was thirty years younger. Other French-born residents of Leon County included Clara Fleeting, married to Georgia-born Richard, who also listed his occupation as farmer. Mary Ann Hoc was age sixty-three, and her merchant son Alfredo was living with her. Some historians say Sebastian Sanguinette and his wife, Marianne, divorced in 1846 and that the court awarded their Frenchtown property to her. She appeared on the 1850 Census as the head of household at age forty-two with no listed occupation, although she was taking care of two boys: fourteen-year-old Julien and eleven-year-old Augustus Nash. Clement Sellier (sometimes seen as Cellier) was a barkeeper with a wife who was from North Carolina and two children who had both been born in Florida. Anthony Maige does not appear on the 1850 Census, but he is listed on the slave schedule as the owner of two slaves: a male, age forty-eight, and a female, age fifty. Josephine Vingerhoets was the last of the Leon County residents listed as having been born in France. Her Dutch husband, Gerarde, had a cabinet shop. In all, these French men and women represented just seven households.

If the numbers do not substantiate naming the community after the origin of its primary residents, where could the name have come from? One theory stems from memories of the War of 1812. A famous battle took place alongside the Raisin River at Frenchtown, Michigan. It was a costly and bloody confrontation. Initially, American regulars and Kentucky volunteers easily routed the British from their tiny fort, but the English gathered more troops from outlying areas, counterattacked and soundly defeated the Americans. When the British moved on, they took walking prisoners with them, but left the wounded to fend for themselves. During the night, Indian supporters of the British massacred over fifty of those Americans left behind. The Americans subsequently used the incident as a rallying cry. "Remember Frenchtown" became as famous as "Remember the Alamo" and "Remember Pearl Harbor" did in later years. This incident would have been widely known, especially to two of Tallahassee's most influential residents, James Gadsden and Robert Butler.

Another tantalizing theory of the origin of the name Frenchtown connects to Hunterdon County, New Jersey, where a city named Frenchtown was formed in the late 1700s. The community had strong abolitionist leanings and was the home of several supporters of the African Methodist Episcopal (AME) Church that was formed in Pennsylvania in 1794. AME ministers made numerous trips into north Florida at the end of the Civil War and may have told stories about the early efforts of the people of Frenchtown to end slavery. Newly freed slaves could have named their Tallahassee home in honor of such a place. Frenchtown, New Jersey, was also the hometown of Perez Brokaw. He was an early settler in Tallahassee who ran a livery stable and had other business interests in town. Brokaw appears on the 1850 Leon County Census but not on the list of slave owners. Either reference could explain the original source of the name.

Perez Brokaw posed for this 1875 portrait with his wife Elizabeth Amanda Tatum Keen. Brokaw died soon after the couple was photographed. *Photo courtesy of the Florida State Archives Photo Collection.*

There is one more possible explanation for the naming of Frenchtown and it is the simplest of them all. The local mulatto carpenter Jourdan Frenchy most likely built several homes in the neighborhood. It is certainly plausible that locals casually referred to the community as "Frenchy's Town" and the name was later shortened in conversation.

Whatever the origin of the name, we know that Frenchtown has always been home to small business owners, tradesmen and blue-collar workers. We also know that it has been predominantly occupied by persons of color since the time of the Civil War.

Chapter 4

PASSAGES

I f Frenchtown *was* named for the few persons of French birth who lived there, it never had the architectural character of cities like New Orleans or looked like the old-world communities from which some of the original settlers came. The community was laced with substantial but unpretentious homes and the simple dwellings that housed their slaves. It was home to skilled tradesmen who worked as carpenters, bakers and watchmakers. Free black and slave women alike did laundry, cooked, acted as nursemaids and performed the chores required to keep larger homes in proper order. Men of color were carriage drivers, livery workers and farm laborers.

Almost every dwelling had a garden of some sort, though most of the yards were nothing more than dirt that was swept clean. Homes and yards were decorated with an occasional flowerbox or patch of blooming foliage. There were no streets paved with bricks or stone, and the region's summer rains most assuredly turned pathways into small streams. In dry weather, wagons, horses and people would have raised billows of red-clay dust into the air.

A typical day's activities would have created a fair amount of noise. Wagon and carriage wheels would have rumbled on packed soil and the voices of those speaking in foreign languages or heavily accented English would have mingled with the sounds of children playing and livestock protesting their captivity. On Sundays, you could have heard the bells tolling from nearby churches.

Churches were important in more ways than one to the early residents of Tallahassee. They served both the spiritual and social needs of the community and provided buildings for all manners of gatherings. The Methodists were the first to establish a foothold, followed by the Presbyterians and Episcopalians. All of them constructed substantial buildings of varying simplicity or opulence. Some of these congregations invited sponsored slaves to belong and attend services. Persons of color were seated in segregated balconies, but many of their names do appear in official records of membership and baptisms.

The first Methodist church in Tallahassee was built in 1825. It was a simple wood structure. There were openings for windows but no glass panes; instead, they were covered by heavy shutters. Church records for the year 1828 indicate there were twenty-seven white members and fifty-two colored. Josiah Evans served as the first pastor. Several others followed, but none of them served for any great length of time. In 1836 the Methodist church sent Reverend Joshua Knowles to assume the pastorship. At the time, Knowles had been a minister for slightly fewer than three years. He was filled with enthusiasm, pleased at the warm greeting he received and grateful for the temporary lodging supplied to him by local merchant William Maner and his large family. Knowles had a penchant for recording observations about his work and wrote that he performed his first wedding ceremony the first Sunday following his arrival. Knowles complained that the congregation was "frequently annoyed by reports of Indian advances or depredations" and he took steps to post sentinels to keep watch. He took great delight in ministering to the black members of his small flock. The church was unfinished, but it still had "a gallery for the colored people, from which came frequently inspiriting responses to enliven the services."

The Episcopalians of the town organized their first church in 1829. Their membership included some of the most prosperous planters in the area. Governor William Duval was a founding member, as were other families of influence, including Bronough, Call, Eppes, Parkhill, Macomb and Betton. The Demilly family joined, but there were no known members of color. In 1837 the congregation built a beautiful brick structure and named it St. John's. Prince Murat pronounced it was "the finest of them all."

The Presbyterians established their church in 1832 under the direction of evangelist Joseph Stiles. The congregation was numbered at eighteen, and two of them were ruling elders. Nonetheless, this small group included several men of wealth. Trustees included John C. Gamble, who was a planter and would-be banker; attorney George Ward; the druggist, Elijah B. Perkins; and several other businessmen. In short order, they raised huge sums of money and built an impressive church at the corner of McCarty (present-day Park Avenue) and Adams Streets. The final tab for initial construction came to just over $13,000—a sum that would translate to just under $295,000 in 2005 dollars. The building had a gallery, but church members ran out of money before it could purchase pews for that area.

Until 1858, visiting Baptist preachers held services in facilities borrowed from the Presbyterians or the Methodists. According to Bertram H. Groene, author of *Ante-Bellum Tallahassee*, William B. Johnson was one of the preachers who traveled about north Florida in the early days. Johnson wrote that the nearest Baptist church was some distance from town and that "the Baptists are few in number and have no meeting house" in Tallahassee. The first Baptist church in Tallahassee proper was built on a lot purchased from a local lodge at the south side of College Avenue.

Susan Bradford Eppes (1846–1942) offered some other thoughts on the practice of religion in early Tallahassee. Susan was the daughter of Dr. Edward Bradford and Martha Lewis Henry Branch. Her grandfather was John Branch, who served as Florida's territorial governor from 1844 to 1845. Branch had also served as North Carolina's governor from 1817 until 1820. Susan married Nicholas Ware Eppes, a man who was socially and politically well connected in his own right. Mrs. Eppes kept a personal journal of her life in Florida's backwoods, wrote three books and established a reputation as a historian of some note. According to Groene, Susan believed that many of Tallahassee's black residents subscribed to and adopted voodoo beliefs and traditions. Whether or not her contention was true, Eppes wrote about one incident when black residents called upon a "Kinjur" man to solve a local mystery. Five Negro children were found dead and the alleged voodoo priest was called upon to determine who was guilty of the apparent murder. Groene quoted Eppes, who wrote, "The priest finally located the witch who had killed the children by means of a spell. He was then said to have drawn an evil, offending lizard from the head of the witch and justice was served." There is little doubt that some of Tallahassee's slaves may have been brought from the Caribbean or might have had familial ties to the area, but it seems unlikely there were voodoo ceremonies being conducted on a widespread basis. If three hundred slaves had congregated together to witness such a trial, it would have been contrary to prevailing law and would have generated great fear among the whites, who would have assumed the event was nothing less than a precursor to a major slave insurrection. Many slaves *were* superstitious. There were those living among them that possessed a great deal of knowledge about natural remedies and who claimed some degree of supernatural skill. The "Kinjur" man was probably Mrs. Eppes's fantasized version of someone her slaves believed had the power to "conjure up" various and sundry ways to ward off real and imaginary threats to the black population. In any case, it is unlikely that Mrs. Eppes would have had firsthand knowledge of the inner workings of the slave community.

Even if some of the bonded people living in Frenchtown believed in voodoo magic, far more of them practiced the Christian faith. Many of them were members of established churches in town and—whether or not they had respect for the "Kinjur" man—they developed a much closer kinship with the Reverend James Page.

Page was born into slavery in Richmond, Virginia, in 1807. He was owned by Colonel John Parkhill, who was among the first wealthy planters to move his primary residence to north central Florida. In 1835 Parkhill married Lucy Randolph, daughter of Thomas Eston Randolph. The Randolphs were allied through marriage to the influential Cary and Eppes families. All of them could trace their American roots back to colonial times. Parkhill was a strong proponent of slavery and was one of the largest slaveholders in the county. However, he did not subscribe to the common practice of forbidding his slaves to openly and freely express their religious beliefs. He built a small church for them on his plantation. In order to comply with Florida's law against slaves congregating in groups without white supervision, Parkhill or one of his family members would attend services with them. He often said he was impressed with the Christian devotion

Reverend James Page was the first pastor to serve at the Bethel AME Church. He led the congregation from 1870 until 1883. *Photo courtesy of the Florida State Archives Photo Collection.*

exhibited by his bonded men and women. James Page showed an early inclination for preaching and Parkhill indulged his talents at every opportunity. James was trained as a gardener and a carriage driver and was a body servant to Colonel Parkhill, but he was allowed to travel from one Leon County plantation to another and is credited with having baptized hundreds of slaves. After the Civil War, the Parkhill family relocated to their summer home at Bel Air, some four miles south of Tallahassee. They set aside some land for Reverend Page to build a "real" church. Volunteers from the area helped to build the new meetinghouse and it was named Bethlehem Baptist Church. James was understandably proud of the little church, but he still wanted to reach people who could not come to him, so the Parkhills kept a horse and buggy at their stable that James could use whenever he wanted.

The Saint James Church was also an anomaly in the antebellum South. John Gilmore Riley attended services there as a young boy. In 1947, at the age of almost ninety-three, he sat down and penned a history of Saint James. Riley wrote that the church was established sometime around 1845 and was operated under the auspices of Trinity Methodist "as a place of worship for the slaves who believed and practiced the Methodist Doctrine." Riley noted that there were no other white churches that had made such a provision. Pastors from Trinity would deliver sermons every Sunday afternoon. Reportedly, the preachers took great delight in preaching to the colored people, who "often shouted and praised God under the red-hot gospel." John added, "People were not afraid of too much enthusiasm for God in those days." Control of the church was gradually turned over to black ministers after the Civil War, but the women of Trinity continued to give singing lessons to the younger members of the congregation. Saint James affiliated with the Christian Methodist Episcopal (CME) church and had one of the largest congregations in town until, as Riley put it, a "mighty disruption" occurred by the "carrying away of 125 of its members by a shrewd politician, Robert Meacham, to form Bethel A.M.E. Church." To this day in 2006, people still debate who was right and who was wrong in making the decision to stay at Saint James or join Robert Meacham at the newly established Bethel. Meacham was a self-proclaimed minister from Jefferson County of considerable influence who did have political aspirations. He subsequently served in the Florida Senate from 1868 to 1879.

While a strong faith guided and supported the people of Tallahassee, it did not protect them from all harm. In 1841 a yellow fever epidemic spread from one port city to the next along the coast of the Gulf of Mexico. Both Apalachicola and St. Marks offered sanctuary for infected sailors, and the disease quickly spread to Leon County. Hundreds died and there was scarcely a family that escaped the fever's wrath. The town's doctors were overwhelmed. Some of the churches were turned into makeshift hospitals. The pastor of the Presbyterian church was among the first to die. Other ministers could hardly keep up with the demand for funeral services. The city cemetery quickly filled and another one was platted out near Frenchtown where carriage makers and carpenters met the grim need for a few new hearses and more coffins. In 1840 enumerators identified 11,442 people who called Tallahassee home. A year later, more than 10 percent of them had died of yellow fever.

Some residents fled the area for points north, but the remaining Tallahasseeans pressed on. Two years later, in the month of May, a small fire started at the Washington Hall boardinghouse. It had been a dry season and it was a windy afternoon. Flames consumed the building before volunteers could douse them, and sparks flew through the air. Weeds and grasses on empty lots ignited and fire skipped over rooftops into the trees, then dropped burning branches back on to roofs. The courthouse was spared, as were several brick buildings downtown. The conflagration was finally brought under control near the northern boundary of town. Every store in town was destroyed, but amazingly not one person was killed. The disaster left the townspeople with an important lesson. Building codes were quickly adopted that required structures to be constructed of brick or to be set back one from another. The city was rebuilt with the support of Floridians from as far away as Jacksonville, and Tallahassee was charged with a new kind of energy.

That energy was almost extinguished in September 1873. Long before weather experts started naming hurricanes, a storm of unknown strength wrecked havoc on the city of Tallahassee. Wind and storm surges battered St. Marks to the south and left almost nothing standing in Port Leon. High winds and heavy rains demolished forty homes and caused damage to almost every other structure in town. Most of the cotton crop was ruined. Fifteen cotton gins were destroyed. Corncribs and barns—some already bursting with an early fall harvest—were smashed, along with fences and other farm buildings. Damages were estimated at over $200,000. Today, that figure would equate to over $3 million. Two people were known to have lost their lives in the storm, but it is likely far more died in outlying areas.

Chapter 5

THE CHANGING FACE
OF TALLAHASSEE

Florida became a state in 1845. New residents continued to flock to the area. Cotton was king and landowners were making money. Planters bought and imported slaves from human auction houses in New Orleans, Charleston and cities in neighboring Georgia. Local dealers brought slaves down from Virginia and tried to smuggle some in from outside the country. Local trades and purchases of bonded individuals were negotiated at widely advertised sales. Children were being born, elder settlers were passing away and life was returning with some semblance of predictability. Meanwhile, the rift between the industrial-based North and the slaveholding agricultural South was growing wider. Despite the warnings of elder statesmen, cautious merchants and residents with family ties in the North, Florida politicians voted to secede from the Union and join the new Confederacy in January of 1861. Richard Keith Call—a man who had enthusiastically promoted Tallahassee to the agents of Lafayette and some of the most powerful families of Virginia and the Carolinas—warned delegates they had "opened the gates of Hell, from which shall flow the curses of the dammed which shall sink you to perdition."

Tallahassee had the distinction of being the only Confederate capital city that did not fall to Union hands during the Civil War. That is not to say the city did not suffer greatly. Call's dismal prediction did come true. Much of Leon County's wealth and agricultural bounty had been diverted to the war effort. Many slaves were pressed into service as personal aides for their masters riding off to war or were sent to Florida-based forts to shore up military emplacements. Hundreds were "leased out" to the Confederacy for sums of two to twenty-five dollars—paid to their owners. Clothing items, medicines and specialty foods such as coffee were in short supply. The few items that made it past Union

blockades cost more than most could afford. Confederate dollars continually dropped in value. News was slow, but dispatches carried word of beloved family members lost on faraway battlefields. Soldiers who were not severely wounded in early battles returned home with missing or shattered limbs from later campaigns.

When President Lincoln signed the Emancipation Proclamation on January 1, 1863, it was essentially ignored in Tallahassee. As the war dragged on, rumors of freedom circulated within the slave community, and some seized the opportunity to head for the

42

This striking monument sits near the entrance to Natural Bridge Historic State Park in honor of all those who fought and died there. The one-day battle claimed the lives of 174 Union and 26 Confederate soldiers. Casualties from both sides were brought to Tallahassee for burial. *Photo by J. Hare.*

perceived protection of Union lines. Some runaways took refuge in the woods around the city and were accused of conducting clandestine raids on outlying plantations. The local newspaper warned residents to "protect themselves" from these dangers. Fears of slave unrest, further deprivations and assaults grew. Volunteer patrols rode though the area trying to round up "offenders" who were often beaten severely. Union forces did make one attempt to attack the city from the Gulf. An estimated nine hundred Union soldiers landed at St. Marks in 1864 and began a march toward the city. News of their arrival traveled faster than the troops. A contingent of young boys from Tallahassee's West Florida Seminary and a gathering of veterans from previous wars were assembled by the few militiamen left in town and they headed south. The two forces met at Natural Bridge some six or seven miles from the city. In spite of the odds against them, the Tallahassee contingent repulsed the Union attack. There was a brief moment of jubilation, but most Southerners felt the die had already been cast and the end of the Confederacy was fast approaching. No one was more despondent than Florida's governor, John Milton. He traveled to his home in Marianna in March of 1865, placed a gun to his head and committed suicide. Word of his death stunned Floridians. They barely had time to mourn his loss when word of Lee's surrender reached the Southland. The news was met with great sadness, but it was tempered with a degree of relief that the war was finally over.

On May 20 of 1865, Union troops, led by Brigadier General Edward McCook, rode into Leon County and commandeered a downtown Tallahassee home. Confederate flags were taken down and the American flag was raised. Eyewitnesses reported that the Third United States Colored Infantry was there to parade their colors and a military band played "John Brown's Body" for all to hear. Local residents, including some slaves, gathered to hear what McCook had to say. He read the Emancipation Proclamation to the assembled crowd and firmly ordered a contingent of soldiers to ride out into the countryside to notify bondsmen they were now free. In-town slaveholders were instructed to immediately inform those in their keeping. The surrender of Confederates to the Union was relatively calm and was treated with dignity and honor on both sides. Predictably, the event caused quite a stir and the practical effect was immediate. Overnight, planters—whose wealth had been measured in part by the number of slaves they owned—found themselves in another world. There was jubilation on one side and a great gnashing of teeth and wringing of hands on the other, but there were no riots. Some planters tried to keep the news from their slaves, hoping to keep them around long enough to harvest the summer crops, but the news spread quickly and work came to an abrupt halt. Four days later, the newspaper observed, "The Negroes are behaving badly." The editor did not clearly define exactly what that meant.

Confederate soldiers were pardoned and slowly made their way back home. Some of the once-wealthy planters and sons of planters returned on horses spent by years of hard riding and poor nutrition. Most former farmers, tradesmen and laborers arrived on foot. Some hobbled home propped up on makeshift crutches or were supported by surviving comrades. Most of them were dressed in tattered clothing; they were dirty, disheveled and disheartened. All of them returned to a world turned upside down from the one they had left four years before. John Demilly, believed to be a direct descendant of one of the Frenchmen who moved to Tallahassee in the 1830s, was among them. In the book *Trinity United Methodist Church 1824–1999*, author Linda Yates quoted a letter John had written during a short leave he had taken during the conflict: "A few days back, I reached Tallahassee. The town was crumbling into decay. The people looking as death itself had encompassed them in its icy chills. The companions of my youth…scattered to the four quarters of the Confederacy." One can't help but wonder how many of his childhood companions never returned. The lucky ones who did survive certainly found a more subdued city than the one that sent them off to war waving flags and shouting enthusiastic promises that they would be returning triumphantly in a scant few months.

Tallahassee—and Frenchtown in particular—had entered a whole new era. The change did not come about without struggle and further conflict.

President Abraham Lincoln was still fabricating plans to reunite the country when his life was cut short by an assassin's bullet days after the Civil War ended. He dreamed of new opportunities for economic growth and of a country that would apply its laws fairly to all citizens. He planned to welcome Confederate states back into the Union as soon as 10 percent of their respective citizens signed loyalty oaths. From a practical standpoint, welcoming the Southern states back into the fold was not as simple as it sounded.

Opportunists from the North and South alike initiated actions to seize valuable plantation lands. Entities holding existing notes moved quickly to foreclose on properties and call in letters of credit. Slaves were often used as mortgages against property and collateral for loans. Without slaves, there was little that could be done to raise funds. Very few Southerners had Federal dollars and their Confederate money was useless. Potential buyers offered pennies on the dollar. Lincoln's successor, Vice President Andrew Johnson, was indecisive in implementing Lincoln's plans and in developing a strategy of his own. Johnson was not particularly sympathetic to the unfortunate situation of newly freed slaves and was not disposed to backtrack on the statements he made before the war supporting states' rights. He proposed blanket pardons for most Confederates, but demanded that planters who had more than $20,000 in assets before the conflict appeal directly to him for clemency. He took steps to return plantations to their prewar owners but did not set up a solid framework to accomplish the task. There was very little action taken to curb the appetite of those eager to seize power and wealth.

Governors were appointed, and removed, and military officers often took independent action to organize efforts to return everyone to some sort of gainful employment. Plantation owners were instructed to start paying wages or negotiate sharecropping agreements. There was little cash to support employment, so most planters opted to enter into contracts that provided land, seed and farm equipment in exchange for labor and crop shares. Most slaves could neither read nor write, and many made their marks on papers that contained lopsided provisions far different than the ones that had been verbally agreed upon. States were expected to adopt new constitutions, but several of them, including Florida, tried to retain old provisions. At one point, Florida lawmakers suggested language that would preserve the institution of slavery as much as possible. As early as 1865, laws were being passed to institute segregationist policies. By 1866, reconstruction efforts in the South were basically out of control. Martial law was declared in Florida. Military occupation did not end until the state developed a constitutional document acceptable to the federal government. Required laws provided for public schools, modernized the court system, revamped tax laws and guaranteed voting rights to African Americans. Florida officially rejoined the Union in July of 1868.

The woman in this circa 1910 photo is believed to be Mrs. Lucinda Paine. She raised four children on her earnings as a laundress and made sure every one of them went to school. *Photo courtesy of the John G. Riley Center/Museum of African American History & Culture.*

Nellie Franklin was born in Frenchtown and worked as a domestic servant. She was identified as a mulatto in the 1880 Federal Census. *Photo courtesy of the Florida State Archives Photo Collection.*

This unidentified man sported a satin-faced coat and carried a fancy walking cane. He was representative of the vital and prosperous black middle class that developed in Tallahassee during the Reconstruction era. *Photo courtesy of the Florida State Archives Photo Collection.*

A few ex-slaves received parcels of land from their former owners. Many of them had no idea how to legally register these "gifts" but took possession of the land nonetheless. In some isolated cases, white property owners simply packed up their belongings and moved away, leaving homes to anyone bold enough to claim them or brazen enough to simply move in. Ex-slaves were initially giddy with their new freedom, but quickly realized they now had to fend for themselves. Hundreds headed out for other areas and dozens of them returned. The 1870 Federal Census was the first to include persons of all races. It is difficult, but not impossible, to scan the fifty-one pages it took to record the names of all the Tallahassee residents to determine precisely which ones lived in Frenchtown proper. One thing that is evident is that whites, blacks and mulattos seemed to be living all over the city, not just in clusters. Daniel Smith, a black carpenter, lived next door to Thomas Ford, who was white and worked as a watchman. Leonard Demilly was a tanner. His household included two African American women who were identified as servants. Jack Austin, a black teamster, resided next door with his wife and eighteen-year-old daughter—both of whom took in laundry to earn cash.

Most Frenchtown residents continued doing what they had always done—providing household services—but now they could earn wages for doing laundry, cooking, cleaning or performing general or farm labor. Earnings were low, but money was their own to spend or keep. There was ample work for women, but jobs for men were harder to come by. The more enterprising among them opened businesses as diverse as fish markets and dressmaking shops. John and Maria Demilly, who were both white, moved from Frenchtown to a large home on Monroe Street when John was appointed to serve as the new county treasurer. Frenchtown residents soon included both the prosperous and the nearly down-and-out.

The Reconstruction Act, passed by Congress in 1867, gave black men the right to vote and hold office. Perhaps the most significant aspect of the legislation is that it also authorized public education for newly freed slaves. Most Southern states had specifically prohibited teaching slaves to read or write, although there were some notable exceptions. Virginia had not enforced such provisions and Tallahassee was fortunate to have several slaves who had learned these important skills and were more than willing to pass them on any way they could. Several members of the Wells and Vaughn families were among the first to step forward publicly to teach.

Though public education for white children had been federally encouraged and supported since 1787, most communities in Florida had made very little effort to build public schools. The majority of white children were taught by hired tutors at selected plantations and private academies, or they were sent to boarding schools in established areas outside the state. The first free whites-only public school opened in Tallahassee in 1850. Only boys over the age of seven could attend. The West Florida Seminary, forerunner of today's Florida State University, opened in 1857 on land adjoining Frenchtown. Both boys and girls over the age of seven could attend—providing they were white and their families could afford the required tuition.

By the time African Americans were granted the right to secure an education, there were few effective models for them to follow. Congress created the Bureau of Refugees,

Freedmen and Abandoned Lands to help with efforts to rebuild the South. Its charge was to offer immediate assistance to emancipated slaves by distributing food and clothing, help them to secure housing and jobs and to act as an advocate for freed slaves in matters of law. In addition, they were to take an active role in establishing a system of education.

Northern teachers were brought in under the protection of the military. Several benevolent societies, such as the African Civilization Society and branches of the African Methodist Episcopal (AME) Church, offered assistance. The local Methodist church offered classes. John Gilmore Riley, who was just eight years old at war's end, was among the first to attend. By the end of 1866, there were a number of schools for blacks operating in Leon County. Accommodations were made to compensate for age and circumstance. Adults were often taught at the plantations where they still lived and some classes were held at night.

"Aunt" Memory Adams was born in Virginia about 1830 and was one of the freed slaves to take full advantage of new opportunities. She was brought to Tallahassee in 1846 and reportedly sold to merchant John W. Argyle for $800. Argyle was from Virginia, and it is quite possible that Memory belonged to him prior to coming to Florida. In either case, she was the only slave that appeared on his entry in the 1850 slave schedule. Argyle died sometime before 1860 and Memory was inherited by his wife, Susan Claxton, who continued to live in their Frenchtown home. Memory had never learned to read or write but wanted desperately to acquire these skills. The 1870 Census indicates she did not know how to do either, but by 1880 she proudly told the census taker she could do both. At some point, Memory married John Adams, but her husband did not live long and it is believed that Memory continued to work for the Argyle family until Susan's death. In 1893 Memory wanted to travel to St. Louis for the World's Fair. Being a woman of amazing enterprise and resourcefulness, she sold photos of herself and made enough to cover all her expenses. At age sixty-three, she was living in the home of Major R. Walker and was identified as his "servant." Walker's home was located on Boulevard Street (now Martin Luther King Boulevard) in Aunt Memory's familiar Frenchtown.

There were no special requirements to be a teacher in the early days of Reconstruction. Sessions might be led by the wife or daughter of a plantation owner, one of the tutors who once taught only white children or by a freed slave whose skills were not much greater than those of his or her students. The Freedmen's Bureau paid for some of the teachers' meager salaries and provided minimal supplies, but the agency was shut down in 1870. Schools were segregated by common practice if not by actual law. African American Charles A. Pierce was serving as the Leon County superintendent of public instruction but, despite his efforts and the entreaties of influential blacks serving in the legislature, Florida law permitted (but did not require) segregation. A common state school fund was established and distributed in relation to the numbers of people between the ages of four and twenty-one who resided in each county. Schools had to meet certain criteria relating to the number of hours during the day or months of the year they were open, but there were no

"Aunt" Memory Adams was a familiar face to many Frenchtown residents. She was nearing eighty when she posed for this photo in 1900. *Photo courtesy of the Florida State Archives Photo Collection.*

requirements regarding curriculum. There had to be at least one teacher for every fifty students and at least 80 percent of those enrolled had to attend daily.

Tallahassee's Lincoln Academy (later known as Lincoln High School) was one of the first black schools to receive recognition by the state. The school was located near the western edge of town. A cadre of volunteers provided most of the construction labor, and Lincoln was formally dedicated in 1869. The local paper reported that a large group of citizens assembled on the grounds to hear speeches made by the governor, the mayor and other dignitaries. A local reporter lamented that the occasion was used for "political purposes" and that a great deal of the rhetoric was "not very credible." The striking whitewashed wooden school building burned down in 1872. The blame was placed on a student who was assigned to clean out the stoves that heated the two-story structure. He allegedly dumped what he believed to be cold ashes into a container located on the second floor. During the night, they reignited, catching nearby materials on fire. The Colored Hook and Ladder Company responded, but city fire trucks did not. This failure was attributed to the fact that they had "insufficient hoses." The building was not insured. Resources were limited and it took some time before Lincoln could be rebuilt.

A new location was selected at nearby Copeland Street and Park Avenue. It opened in 1876 and served the needs of the black community until 1906. By then, the Florida State College for Women was growing, and they made a successful plea to take over the school to house their music department. Leon County set aside a parcel of land on West Brevard Street in Frenchtown for a third Lincoln High School building. Lincoln thrived at its new location. It was the center of much of the social activity that took place in the community during the early years of the twentieth century and it never lacked good leadership.

When the calendar signaled the arrival of 1900, John Gilmore Riley was forty-three years old. Just a few years before, he had moved his family into a new home about halfway between the county courthouse and the land he had purchased in Smokey Hollow on the east side of town. The young boy who had first learned to read with the help of his Virginia-born aunt and volunteers at the Methodist church had grown up to become a teacher himself. His earliest teaching job was in neighboring Wakulla County. He was paid a very small salary the first year and agreed to stay on for room and board only during the second. Riley moved on to the Hinson School in Gadsden County and taught there for almost five years. He secured a position in Tallahassee, contingent upon his passing the tests necessary to be awarded a "Second Class" teaching certificate from the local school board. He easily accomplished this task and in 1893, John Riley was named principal of Lincoln High School. The institution's reputation for scholarship continued to grow. In 1924 Lincoln was one of the few black schools in Florida to be certified by the Southern Association of Colleges and Secondary Schools.

"Professor" Riley retired in June of 1926 and passed away in 1954. His memory lives on in the elementary school named in his honor just north of Frenchtown and in the John G. Riley Center/Museum of African American History & Culture that is

The fourth Lincoln High School was constructed of brick and was an impressive structure for its day.
Photo courtesy of the Florida State Archives Photo Collection.

Lincoln was the only Frenchtown area high school for students of color from 1869 until 1969. Today, the structure houses a daycare center and is the host location for social and service-oriented activities. *Photo by J. Hare.*

Members of the Bethel AME Church posed together for this 1878 photo. *Image courtesy of the Florida State Archives Photo Collection. The original glass negative was a gift from Malcolm B. Johnson.*

housed in the home he built back in the 1890s. The third Lincoln High School—the one that John had helped to build and that he had loved so much—met the same fate as the original school: it burned down to its foundation. In 1929, the fourth Lincoln High School was built on the same site, this time of brick.

Lincoln continued to be an important lifeline to the community of Frenchtown, but it was the community's churches that anchored its residents to one another and to their associated families living in outlying areas.

In 1869 Reverend Page was entering his third year of service as the pastor of the small church he had built in Bel Air and was still driving his borrowed horse and buggy around the countryside, ministering to those in isolated areas. He was conducting services out of doors or in whatever structure was available, performing baptisms and officiating over weddings and funerals. Page traveled as far north as Thomasville, Georgia, and as far south as Key West. His reputation as a leader and as a man of the highest character had spread across nearly all of Florida, and he was deeply respected by black and white alike.

The following year, Reverend Page moved into Tallahassee and presided over the building of Bethel Missionary Baptist Church. He served the congregation for over thirteen years and witnessed the amazing transformation of Frenchtown during Reconstruction and the advent of the Jim Crow era. Little is known about Page's education, or if he received any formal training at all, but he was remarkably intelligent and well aware of what was happening in the world outside of Leon County. He

Father Joseph Hugon served as Leon County's only Catholic priest for over thirty-seven years. This image was taken sometime between 1885 and 1910. *Photo courtesy of the Florida State Archives Photo Collection.*

had a profound respect for education and encouraged his congregation to take every opportunity to learn and grow. In 1878 he placed an ad in the local paper announcing, "The American Baptist Publication Society of Philadelphia—at its International Sunday School Congress in Atlanta included an exhibit of a large invoice of publications. Folks should contact B. Griffith, Secretary if they want to order any."

While the Methodists and Presbyterians developed early roots in Tallahassee and the Baptists most certainly have had a huge influence on Frenchtown, it was the Catholic Church that first introduced Christianity to the area. Historians claim the first new-world Christmas Mass was celebrated in Leon County by De Soto's expedition forces. Spanish missionaries were here as early as the sixteenth century. The earliest whites to sink down roots in the Red Hills settled on Spanish land grants long before the arrival of the Americans. Some of these people—regardless of their religious leanings—accepted baptism in the Catholic faith because it was politically and socially expedient to do so. From the earliest days of American occupation, white settlers were visited by Catholic priests who operated in much the same way as the Methodist circuit riders who came after them. There were already established dioceses in both St. Augustine and Mobile, Alabama, and we know that many immigrants from East Florida and some that came from France were practicing Catholics.

In 1827 Bishop Portier traveled from Mobile to "minister to those of the faith" living in Tallahassee. In an article written for the *Florida Historical Quarterly*, author Dorothy Van Brunt quotes the bishop, who wrote that it was his "good fortune to celebrate mass there on Sunday, June 23" although where that service took place is unknown. In 1845 Portier returned to Tallahassee and purchased two lots in the Northern Addition. A mostly volunteer labor force built a church that was small by today's standards, but still elegant in its English Gothic style. The Catholics called it Sorrowful Mother. In 1847 the church burned. Parishioners were able to salvage nothing but the church's bell and were unable to rebuild the sanctuary until 1854 when the Church of St. Mary was constructed at the corner of present-day Park Avenue and Gadsden.

One of the earliest known residents of Frenchtown was Jacques Hugon, who may have come from South Carolina via New Orleans, but he was believed to have been born in France. He was in Leon County as early as 1829 when he married Ann C. Goodwin. The family appears on the 1840 Tallahassee Census with four in the household. There was a small boy between the age of five and ten, a female between age twenty and thirty and two adult males, one between twenty and thirty and the other between forty and fifty. Whatever age Jacques was, we presume he was deceased when Ann remarried in June of 1843 to U.H. Niles.

This information may have slipped into the obscurity of one family's genealogy if not for the arrival of Catholic Father J.L. Hugon in 1877. Father Hugon claimed to have been born in France sometime around 1843. His first assignment as a priest was in Key West, Florida, in 1875. In 1877 he moved to Tallahassee and selected Frenchtown as the location for his first parish home. Is it possible he knew about the area because he had a family connection here?

By 1870 the Church had purchased an additional structure at 404 North Monroe for use as a convent. Surely there was a considerable Catholic influence in town to warrant such an investment. The good father walked to St. Mary's every day from his Frenchtown home where Emma Wilson, an elderly African American woman, was enumerated as his resident cook. Emma had been born about 1820 in Georgia and was most likely a former slave. Also in the home were Mary Love, identified as a nurse, who was born sometime around 1862, and a little girl named Ellen Wilson, who was age five in 1880. In 1892 Father Hugon facilitated the construction of a new church at the corner of North Monroe and Carolina. It was named Blessed Sacrament. Hugon was still serving as the parish priest at the time of his death on November 8, 1912. He was buried in the Old City Cemetery and was fondly remembered for his constant efforts to unite Catholics and Protestants, blacks and whites, and both the rich and the poor. The eventual fate of the convent is uncertain.

Chapter 6

Quiet Repression and Quiet Strength

As early as 1865, powerful legislators were already working to repress the rights that had been granted to ex-slaves. The bloody battles of the Civil War had ended, but the new Union was demanding the South adopt policies that many Southerners found difficult, if not impossible, to accept. In addition to providing immediate and direct aid, the Freedmen's Bureau was charged with implementing new guidelines for how freed slaves would transition into the world of commerce and paid employment. Ex-slaveholders saw this dramatic change not only in economic terms but also as a personal attack on their way of life.

Most plantation owners had controlled their labor forces with threats of—or actual—physical punishment, being sold and transported away from family members or other diverse privations. These actions were now illegal or not applicable. Slaves had been provided with various degrees of free housing, medical services, clothing and food. Now that they were free, ex-bondsmen had few ways to secure any of these commodities. Property owners had been left with few resources to pay for labor that had previously been free. The majority of Southerners never owned slaves and were caught squarely in the middle. The poorest among them now had to compete with thousands of new people in the workforce that had not previously affected them one way or the other.

Freedmen's Bureau personnel were expected to sort it all out. Unfortunately, they were unable to satisfy everyone and they were mistrusted on all sides. To ex-slaves, they represented one more division of the white-controlled power system. To former slaveholders, the bureau represented occupation by a former enemy. The agency's powers left them wide open to accusations of misuse of funding, overstepping the limits of their authority, failures to force ex-slaves to work and of being ineffective at delivering much-needed support systems to those without resources. Rumors circulated that former bondsmen would receive "forty acres and a mule" in payment for their years of suffering and a few waited around for that to occur. Plantation owners believed they could—and needed to—continue to control their former property with a strong hand in order to get them to work. Neither concept proved to be true.

According to Joe M. Richardson, who prepared a meticulously researched article on the subject for the *Florida Historical Quarterly*, Tallahassee proper had a particularly difficult time getting ex-slaves back to work. The *Tallahassee Floridian* observed, "Every stable and out house was filled with people who did not work." In response, Freedmen's Bureau Commissioner Oliver O. Howard issued an order in November of 1865 providing that "the usual remedies for vagrancy, breaking of contracts, and other crimes, will be resorted to; the freedmen and other persons of African descent having the same rights and privileges before military and civil courts as the white citizens have." Both owners and laborers could levy complaints against one another through the bureau, but mediation did not always result in contract alterations or fair redress. As a practical matter, it took some degree of time before the dust started to settle.

Freedmen's Bureau agents targeted the north-central areas of the state, making speeches and offering assistance in negotiating labor contracts. Typically, agreements spelled out the necessity of employers to advance a weekly minimum of food to include "four pounds of bacon, a peck of meal, and a pint of syrup" to each worker. In return, the laborer had to agree—in writing—to the number of hours he or she would work. Most times, a worker's wife and older children were also bound by the contract. There was no minimum wage, so most arrangements provided for sharing crops and the expected profits thereof. The bureau was inconsistent in monitoring the fairness of these agreements. One contract, signed in Leon County, required the laborer to "mortgage" the crop as security for payment of rent and other provisions. No part of the crop could be sold until the owner received four hundred pounds of lint cotton for each acre farmed. In a bad year, the laborer earned nothing and was even left in debt for the privilege of having worked. In another instance, the laborer had to pay the owner if he or she was unable to work a day for reasons of illness or other incapacity. In some cases, sharecroppers were allowed to plant small vegetable gardens but were not allowed to harvest any of it for personal use.

Vagrants slowly left Frenchtown and returned to the plantations to work. Some of its white residents left as well. Frenchtown was increasingly identified with former slaves. Nonetheless, small businesses were starting to open up that provided services ranging from shoemaking to shoeing horses and from taking in laundry to tailoring new clothes.

The memory of George Proctor's reprehensible abandonment of his family had faded to some degree. His son, John Elijah Proctor, could not have done much more to restore the family honor. John initially got a job as a waiter at the City Hotel, but by the time he was twenty-six, he was married, had two children and was teaching school. He served in the ministry and was elected to the Florida House of Representatives in 1873, 1875 and 1879. In 1883 he was elected to the Florida State Senate and was reelected in 1885. He was well acquainted with the Frenchtown neighborhood and made frequent visits there to meet with his constituents.

John Proctor was the grandson of Antonio Proctor, a free black man who came to Tallahassee in the 1830s. John was active in politics during the latter part of the nineteenth century. *Photo courtesy of the Florida State Archives Photo Collection.*

John Proctor posed in front of his home on the occasion of his ninety-fifth birthday. His daughter Lettie and an unidentified woman stood nearby. *Photo courtesy of the Florida State Archives Photo Collection.*

Virginia-born, ex-Union soldier and new Tallahassee resident Josiah T. Walls was elected Florida's first U.S. representative to Congress. He completed three terms before the end of Reconstruction. Other African Americans, like Leon County's John Wallace and freeborn Jonathon Gibbs, assumed leadership roles in the state legislature. Gibbs was highly educated. He had apprenticed as a carpenter but later attended Dartmouth College, where his studies included Latin, Greek, mathematics and philosophy. He moved on to Princeton Theological Seminary and subsequently served as a Presbyterian minister. After the Civil War, he opened a school for freemen in North Carolina. The church transferred him to Florida in 1867. The following year, he was elected as a delegate to Florida's Constitutional Convention. Gibbs was probably the most educated representative in attendance. In 1868 Gibbs was appointed to serve as Florida's secretary of state.

Men like Walls, Wallace and Gibbs were Tallahassee residents and they set high standards of confidence and decorum for others to follow. A vibrant black middle class was forming and Tallahassee was managing the transitions of class and economic standing better than most Florida communities. Tallahassee was, after all, a capital city where merchants and laborers, attorneys and farmers all shared the streets with the politically powerful. While these politicians wrangled over new policies and constitutional interpretations at the capitol, Frenchtown experienced an economic boom and its own social revolution.

In March of 1875, Phillip DeCoursey was named sheriff of Leon County. He was a black-skinned man who is believed to have derived his name from the French-born Jean de Corce. Sadly, DeCoursey fell victim to pneumonia less than a year after he took office. The *Weekly Floridian* reported that Phillip was "a member of Rev. James Smith's Southern Methodist Church where he was the Sabbath School Superintendent. A large group of all citizens attended his funeral. He was an honest man, a good citizen, and a faithful officer."

We can learn a great deal about the way Tallahassee felt about its own citizens through articles that were printed in the local newspaper. This obituary notice appeared on January 11, 1876: "HENRY HICKS, a colored mechanic, well known to community of over 30 years (1846) died at his home near the Depot of pneumonia. Ran for Legislature in 1874 with a good showing (independent ticket) and was elected to the City Council in 1875. Peace to his ashes."

Some state-level politicians and their citizen supporters did not share this propensity for neighborly connection and admiration. They felt threatened by the increasing influence of ex-slaves with money and transplanted blacks from the North. Recalcitrant Confederates were still angry over the loss of the war and even more incensed that states were being forced to ram Union policies into newly required constitutions. They were just waiting for the right opportunity to reverse the postwar trend toward social, political and economic equalization of the races.

Jim Crow was an 1830s fictional character, portrayed in a popular minstrel show by a white entertainer named Thomas Rice. Rice would blacken his face with burnt cork, sing an offensive song in dialect and dance about the stage. Some historians believe he patterned the character after having seen a disabled black man dancing in the street. The song "Jump Jim Crow" became a national bestseller in sheet music form. Rice's performance was derogatory at best and beyond cruel at its worst. Before long, the term Jim Crow became a euphemism for blacks who were considered to be lazy and dull-witted. After the war, Jim Crow was the phrase attached to a succession of laws that were passed to subjugate African Americans to the lower levels of society.

Florida passed some of the harshest laws in the South. Railroad cars were segregated. An African American or a mulatto who entered a "white" railroad car was subjected to a punishment of thirty-nine lashes or could be placed in a pillory. A pillory was constructed of hinged boards with cutouts for the head, feet and hands. Persons convicted of crimes would be positioned in them for a period of hours. Some citizens and unruly children would throw vegetables or other things at the offender, who could do nothing to protect himself. By 1873, blacks and whites could no longer share public accommodations. Segregated areas were set up in railway stations, inns, places of entertainment and certainly schools. Laws were adopted to prohibit mixed-race marriages. By 1895 penalties and fines for numerous infractions against segregation laws were strengthened. It became a penal offense for "any person to conduct any school, any grade, either public or private where whites and blacks are instructed or boarded in the same building, or taught in the same class by the same teachers." Conviction could result in fines up to $500 and imprisonment of up to six months. In 1916 three nuns at the Sisters of St. Joseph School in St. Augustine were actually arrested for the offense and the news circulated around the nation. Witnesses reported that the sisters were paraded through the streets like common criminals. The *Cleveland Advocate* (Ohio) printed, "This is the disgrace that today stamps Florida before the eyes of the nation."

Official Reconstruction efforts ended when Rutherford B. Hayes assumed the presidency in 1877. The 1876 election had been questionable at best. Florida delegates were in a position to cast the deciding electoral vote, but there were questions about the legality of ballots and who would be awarded the state's favor. While politicians argued the situation over at the capital, telegraph lines running out of Tallahassee were cut and other news sources were restricted. The Compromise of 1877—in simple terms— allowed Washington Republicans to retain power under a Hayes administration that agreed in advance to withdraw federal monitors from the South and essentially ignore Jim Crow policies. The enforcement of civil rights laws effectively came to a halt.

Many African Americans were removed from public office. Those black male citizens who attempted to vote in subsequent elections were targeted. There were numerous accounts of actions taken against Negroes who wanted to participate in the political process. Some were evicted from their homes, some lost their jobs and brutal attacks and lynchings increased. Between the years 1880 and 1888, 27 percent of the registered black voters stopped going to the polls.

The Fifteenth Amendment guaranteed the right to vote to all Negro men over the age of twenty-one, but many Southern states—Florida included—circumvented federal legislation by passing state laws designed to keep African Americans from voting.

"Grandfather clauses" were adopted that limited voter eligibility to those persons whose grandfathers had voted prior to 1867—effectively eliminating all ex-slaves. State law denied the right to vote to convicted felons, so hundreds of blacks were arrested on flimsy or trumped-up charges. "White primaries" were set up because—technically—political parties were private institutions and therefore not under the jurisdiction of the federal government. Literacy laws were passed that required a potential voter to pass various types of tests before he could cast his vote. Voters could be required to read or interpret portions of the Constitution "to the satisfaction" of the examiner. Most election officials were satisfied with the performance of white citizens, while blacks rarely passed the test. This practice was not officially outlawed until the passage of the 1964 Civil Rights Act. Charging a "poll tax" was another method used to disenfranchise both poor white and black voters. The practical effect was that, just like in the early days of colonial America, voting was effectively limited to wealthy white men. This provision was outlawed in federal elections by passage of the Twenty-fourth Amendment that same year, but the practice did not apply to state elections until the Supreme Court ruled it unconstitutional in 1966. In the interim period of time, things got much worse before they got better.

In 1896, the U.S. Supreme Court heard the case of *Plessy v. Ferguson* and issued a ruling that upheld "separate but equal" policies as being legal within the bounds of the Constitution.

A slave who questioned the fairness of an order issued by his owner faced almost certain punishment. During Reconstruction, there were some limited protections offered to persons of color, but it still took a great deal of courage to speak out against anyone in power. The danger increased as federal influence diminished in the former Confederate states and the end of the nineteenth century drew near. Sharecroppers who questioned whether their portion of the profits was calculated correctly were often thrown off the land with virtually nothing in their hands. Northern companies bought thousands of acres for tobacco and other farming, but they hired local men to run them. There were numerous documented cases in Leon and neighboring counties where the relationship between "farm boss" and "labor" strongly resembled the days of overseer and slave. Beatings for perceived failures to work hard enough or for making comments that were considered back talk were not uncommon. In the worst cases, Negroes were being murdered by both large and small mobs of hate-driven vigilantes. There were more recorded lynchings per capita in the state of Florida between the years 1900 and 1930 than any other state in the country. Not all of the victims were black, but the overwhelming majority of them were. Reports of these atrocities were circulated in the press across the country, but most people felt far removed from the situation. Neither the executive nor legislative branches of the government would adopt anti-lynching laws. Hundreds of African Americans living around Leon County decided the best thing to do was to leave the South and head North, where wages were higher and violence against blacks was reportedly rare. However, local officials were concerned about the potential loss of laborers. At one point in time, Leon County sheriff's deputies actually shut down the railroad station in Tallahassee. The mayor's office asked Northern companies to stop trying to recruit workers. Efforts to keep laborers of color in the area ranged from enlightened offers to increase wages to barbaric beatings. Nonetheless, thousands of black Floridians managed to leave the state during the Great Migration of 1910 to 1930. In 1900, 80 percent of Tallahassee's total population was classified as "B" (black) in the Federal Census. By 1930, that percentage had dropped to 58. Frenchtown residents still remember hearing stories about neighbors and relatives who left home hoping to find a better life in the North.

To those who stayed behind, it was more than obvious that they could not look to local, state or national government for protection. It was also evident that no individual could stand up against old "plantation thinking" or effectively challenge Jim Crow policies. African Americans would have to form support organizations at every level: nationally, in-state and within their own communities.

Lodges and social clubs offered some degree of structure to deal with individual and community problems. Insurance companies were established. African Americans never stopped working toward full equality, but they did recognize that if they were going to be segregated from the community as a whole they would have to take actions to create internal systems to address their common needs. Organizations often served as safe havens and offered an avenue both for advancement and as places where members could be afforded dignity and be treated with respect. Some of these groups operated on a national or state level, but individuals needing immediate help turned to local organizations first.

Most Frenchtown residents knew John Riley as the principal of Lincoln School, but he was also an astute businessman who owned property in several areas of town. He was often seen walking to work, dressed in his trademark suit and tie. On his way back home, he would frequently stop to talk to businessmen in the community. He was affectionately referred to and addressed as "the Professor" and was respected by both black and white Tallahasseeans. Riley believed that securing wealth was the surest path toward respectability, and his personal experience proved his thinking to be correct. He knew that during the Jim Crow years African Americans would never be accepted in local Chambers of Commerce or similar business-support groups, so he encouraged Frenchtown merchants and other black business owners to start an organization of their own. Members called themselves the Tallahassee Development Club (TDC). For several years the TDC acted as an advisory and support group in much the same way as today's professional associations. There were rumors that the TDC also functioned as a liaison between the parallel universes of the segregated city, and there is some limited evidence that supports that contention. Fraternization between blacks and whites was restricted by local ordinance and social custom, but in economic terms, it made good sense for all the businessmen in town to cooperate with one another. Professor Riley allegedly brokered more than one loan agreement between the parties of the first and second part. Meetings were often conducted during the evening hours and in secret. Tallahassee old-timers claim more than one disagreement—about who would conduct what sort of trade from which specified location—was worked out by reasonable men behind closed doors. No one on either side of the racial divide ever lost face under the quiet umbrella of the TDC.

Riley was also a Mason. In simple terms, Freemasons subscribe to a common belief in a Supreme Being and the immortality of the soul. Groups came together to support common interests and functioned as fraternal organizations. Most historians trace the origins of Freemasonry back to seventeenth-century stonemasons in Ireland. The society spread throughout the British Empire, including colonial America. In 1775, eighteen freeborn African Americans were initiated into a Boston Masonic Lodge. Among them was a man named Prince Hall. For a time, the group was given authority to conduct limited work within the Masonic organization. Recognition of American Masonic Lodges was removed during the War of 1812 and later returned. In the process, black Masons were cast aside. Prince Hall and his lodge were unable to align with the new American Masonic structure, so they applied for and received authority from a British Lodge to form the African Lodge No. 459. From that point, Masonic Lodges with black membership were referred to as "Prince Hall" jurisdictions. While they operated in parallel ways to white lodges, there was very little cross-control interaction.

Masonry was respected by both races and there are stories of events that occurred when association membership overrode Southern segregationist policies. Riley joined the Society as a young man and was instrumental in starting the Tallahassee-based St. James No. 26 Holy Royal Arch Masons Chapter in 1902. He helped set up other chapters in neighboring counties and went on to be elected grand high priest of the Florida Arch Masons. After Professor Riley died in 1954, members of his family recalled numerous occasions when he was able to use his Masonic connections to intervene on behalf of one local resident or another. One such incident involved a Frenchtown resident who was accused of having insulted a white merchant. Fearing that he would be killed for the offense, he made his way to Riley's home under cover of darkness and pleaded for help. The Professor was able to broker a deal for the young man. If he would agree to leave town immediately, the Masons would assure him safe passage. The offender agreed to the terms, gathered his personal things, bid farewell to family members and by morning he was safely on his way on the first train headed North.

The Knights of Pythias was founded in Washington, D.C., in 1864 by Justus Henry Rathbone to address the residual effects of the anger and hatred that surfaced during the Civil War. It was a social and fraternal organization grounded in principles of friendship, benevolence and charity. Its motto was "Peace through understanding" and it was the first fraternal order to be chartered by an Act of Congress. Apparently, the organization was more interested in uniting former political enemies than they were in forming friendships that transcended racial lines. In 1869 the organization rejected the petition of a group of black Pennsylvanians to join the group by a vote of twenty-four to eighteen. They would turn down similar requests in 1871, 1878 and 1888. In the meantime, African Americans established a parallel order in 1875 using the same name. Before all was said and done, the original Knights of Pythias would practically self-destruct over internal squabbling and accusations over missing and misspent funds, while the black orders thrived. Arguments over who could legally use the name went all the way to the Supreme Court.

By the second decade of the twentieth century, an estimated 16 percent of Florida's black males belonged to the Knights of Pythias. Members took a public oath to "stand together against racial oppression" and a secret pledge to pay their poll taxes and exercise their right to vote. Initially, members pooled their limited resources to pay for funeral services and provide assistance to the sick and needy among them, but the organization quickly became an integral part of all aspects of life in the black community. The Pythians offered a source of belonging and social connection as well as an avenue for social recognition in the community. At the state and national level, the organization fought more than one legal battle and was a key player in pursuing civil liberties. In Frenchtown, the Knights of Pythias Hall was a place where people felt free to speak out about the challenges of the day and to exchange information about all the events going on in the community. In addition, they sponsored frequent social events.

The African American Life Insurance and Central Life Insurance Companies both had offices in Frenchtown. During the Jim Crow years, it was almost impossible for people of color to obtain insurance coverage. Culturally, it was important to the community to be assured of a proper burial and also to leave some limited funds for loved ones. Insurance companies also provided benefits for workers who were injured on the job or who developed long-term illnesses. Finally, they provided white-collar jobs for people of color.

The National Association for the Advancement of Colored People (NAACP) grew out of concerns about growing racial tensions in the North. A riot that occurred in 1908 in Springfield, Illinois, shocked the nation and led William English Walling to write an editorial demanding that "we must come to treat the Negro on a plane of absolute political and social equality." His words inspired Mary White Ovington, who contacted Walling and others she felt would support the cause of justice. The NAACP was formally set up in 1909 by a multiracial group of influential and concerned citizens and claims the distinction of being America's oldest civil rights organization. The group had members in Florida, but they were not very active within the state until the 1930s. The Tallahassee chapter was not formally established until after troops returned from World War II. The NAACP advocated for change in a multitude of ways, including providing legal representation, facilitating voter registration and helping to pass civil rights legislation.

Florida civil rights activists and African American leaders gathered in 1919 to discuss ways they could work together within the state. The result was the formulation of a group that named itself the Negro Uplift Association (NUA). Members agreed they would work together to end lynching and other brutal practices aimed at individuals. At the same time, they vowed to work for positive gains in education and employment. The NUA was structured to allow members to elect delegates at the local level. Most of the men who were elected were well-known leaders in their own communities and often belonged to several black organizations. In May of 1919, the group approached the Florida Senate with a petition that asked for action on such issues as lengthening the school year and improving the conditions of segregated waiting rooms at railroad depots. In addition, the petition asked for recognition of the contributions of black soldiers who had fought for their country during World War I. The Florida Senate not only refused to include the petition in its official journal, but they also stopped the clerk midway through its reading. The event was widely reported. The *Cleveland Advocate* printed the story in its May 24 issue and considered the incident "one of the worst insults ever perpetrated."

On the steamy night of July 19, 1937, two young African American boys were stopped by a white Tallahassee police officer who suspected them of having broken into a business on South Adams Street. His took them into custody and at some point someone produced a knife. In the ensuing scuffle, the officer said he was stabbed by one or both of them. The boys fled on foot, leaving the bleeding policeman behind. Within an hour, the officer was in the hospital and the boys had been recaptured. Richard Ponder and Ernest Hawkins were locked up in the Leon County Jail. They were questioned for hours by Tallahassee Police Chief Gid Powledge, Leon County Sheriff Frank Stoutamire and State Attorney Orion Parker, all of whom swore the boys confessed to both the attempted robbery and the knifing. Official records identified both Ponder and Hawkins as each being age eighteen, but neighbors claimed they were barely fourteen.

The next day, the *Tallahassee Democrat* reported that the officer was in "fair" condition. Later that night, after a series of questionable actions on the part of the police, four men with masked faces managed to get the two boys out of the jail and into a waiting car. They were driven three miles east of town and shot multiple times. The incident ignited fear and anger in the African American community and garnered national interest as one of the most shocking lynching incidents of its time. Governor Cone opened an investigation that subsequently cleared the Tallahassee Police Department and the Leon County Sheriff's office of any complicity in the brutal murder. No one was ever arrested for the crime.

It was only logical that the Frenchtown community would start to close ranks, not only to assure its economic well-being but for protection.

Chapter 7

Fair Is Fair: Civil Rights

Students of the modern civil rights movement tend to focus on events that occurred during the decades of the fifties and sixties, but the struggle for equality among the races has been ongoing since the founding of America. Perhaps some of the most significant protests against Jim Crow laws and segregationist policies took place when the United States went to war in 1941. At that point, no one could have anticipated that the tiny community of Frenchtown would play a major role in changing federal policies relating to the military.

America was ill prepared for war when the Japanese bombed Pearl Harbor. The country needed trained men and equipment as quickly as possible. Existing bases were expanded and new training facilities were hastily built. The tiny Gulf-side fishing community of Carrabelle was selected as the site for Camp Gordon Johnston. Troops were also brought into Tallahassee and billeted at Dale Mabry Airfield. At the beginning of the conflict, America's military was segregated. Recruiting ads shouted, "We Want You!" and millions of men of all colors stepped forward. The Marine Corps had been exclusively white for well over 150 years, but in 1942 the United States created a Marine Corps Negro Battalion that offered opportunities and specialized training for "barbers, cooks, bakers, clerks and truck drivers."

At its height, Camp Gordon Johnston stretched over 100,000 acres, and between 1942 and 1946, the post was "home" to more than 225,000 military personnel. The encampment earned a well-deserved reputation for being just about the worst place a soldier could be stationed. Even the nation's surgeon general pronounced it an "unhealthy" site. There was very little to do during off-duty hours. A service club, library and guesthouse were built, but only for use by white personnel. Minority soldiers could go fishing or engage in an occasional baseball game, but there was very little else to do on base. Tallahassee, some sixty miles away, was the closest city with hotels, restaurants, theaters and musical entertainment. Even though Leon was officially "dry" until 1949, Tallahassee offered far more diversion than Carrabelle, and soldiers seemed to be able to secure liquor anyway by some unknown means. Arrangements were made for buses to run from the base to town and back again, so the city was the logical place to go on a weekend night. Eventually, a rail line was constructed between Camp Gordon Johnston and Tallahassee and the visits increased. One USO center was set up for white soldiers and another one was opened for soldiers of color. Mabry Airfield was close by. Soldiers stationed there could avail themselves of the city's entertainment even more frequently. In fact, soldiers from Gordon Johnston complained that the men at Mabry would book up all available hotel rooms and get to all the restaurants and nightspots long before they could travel from Carrabelle. The job of maintaining control of military personnel visiting from both places was assigned to the Military Police (MP) units stationed at Mabry.

The MPs expected to deal with the usual cases of drunken privates or a few soldiers itching for a street fight, but they faced an additional challenge that required more diplomatic skill than brute force. Black soldiers, many of them having arrived from the North, ran headlong into Florida's Jim Crow policies of segregation. The famed college-educated Tuskegee Airmen (who practiced their bombing runs and gunnery missions at Mabry) were among them. Benjamin O. Davis Jr., America's first African American Air Force general, later recalled, "We had not been expecting much in the way of hospitality at Dale Mabry, but it sent a chill through us to learn we were to stay in a building that had been used as a guardhouse for black prisoners." Uniformed or not, African Americans were expected to frequent only those restaurants and theaters located in the predominantly black areas of town and that usually meant Frenchtown. Still, some military personnel refused to ride in the back of local buses or confine themselves to using the facilities indicated for "Colored Only." There were several occasions when the MPs had to be called in to settle down an unhappy soldier or quell minor disturbances. In August of 1944, the military sent in African American MPs and they were in no mood to exercise diplomacy. During an attempted arrest, they severely beat one of the offenders and his fellow soldiers rioted. Before all was said and done, civilian police moved in with tear gas and weapons. Two more incidents occurred in October. The first altercation began when a local white police officer tried to arrest a black soldier from Gordon Johnston. Later in the evening, a fight broke out among six drunken enlisted men. When a full force of black MPs tried to take them into custody, others jumped to their defense and a spirited fracas ensued.

Mayor Malcolm Yancy protested and the military commander at Camp Johnston cancelled leave privileges for all of his men. The order stood for many weeks, but it proved difficult to keep such a large group of men confined on base and the ban was soon lifted. In August of 1945, things really got out of hand when a group of nearly 250 black soldiers from both bases started a full-blown riot in Frenchtown. They threw bottles and anything else they could pick up, damaged several black-owned businesses and battled repeatedly with both the military and civilian police forces. Before the evening was over, military personnel had ventured away from Frenchtown's commercial district and entered its residential neighborhood. Some of the participants later claimed they were under stress from having received orders to ship out for overseas assignments and simply wanted to "paint the town red" that night. Most people believed that anger over segregationist policies was the real reason tempers boiled over during that long hot summer. In either case, it took all available military police units, officers from the local police department and some hastily called highway patrolmen to quell the disturbance. While there was considerable property damage, no one was injured and only the MPs made any arrests. The military investigated the incident, but their findings were never made public.

There is no doubt that the residents and business owners of Frenchtown and Tallahassee in general benefited economically from the influx of military personnel, but when the two bases were phased out toward the end of the war there was a selective sigh of relief in Leon County. The nightclub owners were disappointed, but ladies' church societies were delighted. Saturday nights were much quieter and relative calm settled over the community—until the veterans came home.

Like the rest of the nation, Frenchtown celebrated the men and women that returned from World War II and mourned those that had not. Seventy-six of Tallahassee's finest had left to fight and never returned. In his book *Emancipation Betrayed*, author Paul Ortiz wrote that flyers announcing the event proclaimed, "The great welcome home celebration for colored soldiers of Leon County will take place Tuesday, May 20th, at Bethel Baptist church at 4 o'clock." It is interesting that the day set aside to commemorate emancipation in Leon County was the same one selected to celebrate the return of its black fighting men.

Soldiers on both sides of the race coin returned older, wiser and with a different attitude. Some veterans found jobs, some took advantage of the 52/20 program (so named because vets could receive twenty dollars per week for fifty-two weeks until they made the transition back to civilian life) and some wanted to take advantage of the new GI Bill. In 1947 the Florida Legislature declared that the Florida State College for Women should be a co-ed institution and changed the name to Florida State University. Freshman enrollment almost doubled and that meant there were twice as many new neighbors living next door to Frenchtown. Florida A&M University (FAMU) experienced similar increases. The GI Bill opened the door to thousands who would not have been able to afford college otherwise.

During the course of the war, black soldiers had exhibited dignity under difficult circumstances and bravery under brutal fire. They had earned the gratitude and admiration of their communities. The Tuskegee Airmen and other black units had proven the myth about the "inferiority" of the African race to be blatantly false. Over 12 percent of America's World War II troops were African American. Along with their Native American and Latino counterparts they demanded the right to vote without interference. Veterans organized drives to change Jim Crow laws and joined organizations that advocated their cause. During the course of the war, the National Association for the Advancement of Colored People (NAACP) increased its national membership from just fewer than fifty thousand to over five hundred thousand. Many of the civil rights efforts led by GIs failed at local and state levels but in 1948, under a great deal of public pressure, President Franklin Roosevelt officially ended segregation in the U.S. military.

The wartime incidents in Frenchtown helped to change unfair policies within the military, but that was just the beginning of Tallahassee's role in the continuing fight to change Jim Crow attitudes in the rest of the nation.

In 1956 Tallahassee was feeling the effects of America's postwar prosperity. The city had grown to 38,000 and although one third of them were of African descent, segregation was a very real part of everyday life. During an oral history Laura Dixie recorded for the John G. Riley Center/Museum of African American History and Culture, she related a story that illustrates the personal impact of Jim Crow. Laura was getting ready to graduate from Lincoln High School. Her teacher offered to take Laura and five or six of her classmates shopping for dresses for the occasion. They went downtown, entered a popular department store and started to look around. It wasn't long before store clerks took the teacher aside and the girls were instructed to "go outside and wait." Soon, the teacher joined them. She was crying. Though she tried to make up some story regarding why they had to leave, the girls pressed her for the truth. She told Laura and the other girls they would not be allowed to try on any dresses. Either the teacher (who appeared to be white) could model them or they could make an outright purchase, but they could not try the dresses on. In an interview conducted with Reverend Edwin Norwood Jr. by the *Tallahassee Democrat*, he commented that adults protected young people from "the indignities of segregation." Surely that was what Laura's teacher was trying but failed to do.

During the days of Reconstruction, Tallahassee residents of all colors had shared neighborhoods, and—even if there were clearly defined class and economic lines—city dwellers exchanged a mutual respect that helped the town to grow. Jim Crow laws forced the community to divide and take sides. Black families were primarily living in Frenchtown, Smokey Hollow or in the Bond Community. No bank would write them a mortgage in a "white" neighborhood, which really did not matter because no realtor or private seller would have shown them such a house anyway.

Racially motivated violence during the early part of the twentieth century had fostered hatred and mistrust on both sides. While some citizens advocated change, others spoke out against it. On one hand, the city recruited and hired two black policemen and built a "black" golf course and a swimming pool—on the other hand, there was an ordinance on the books that prohibited blacks and whites from associating with one another. The law was actively enforced.

On a national level, the cause for equal rights took a leap forward in 1954 when the U.S. Supreme Court ruled that the "separate but equal" principles set forth in *Plessy v. Ferguson* were unconstitutional. The highest court in the land ruled in *Brown v. the Board of Education* that public schools would have to integrate. Unfortunately, the court did not set forth a time frame.

The state of Florida moved at a snail's pace. The Leon County School District did not start desegregating until 1967. Instead of busing children from one corner

Lincoln students gathered in the school library in this photo taken in the 1940s. Students were expected to come to class "dressed in a manner appropriate for young ladies and gentlemen." *Photo courtesy of the Florida State Archives Photo Collection.*

of the county to another, some schools were closed down entirely and many African American teachers were dismissed in the process. Blacks were promised access to better school facilities, newer textbooks and more opportunity. There was also a downside. African American children lost the support systems and protections afforded them by schools and teachers who understood the unique problems many of them faced. Most kids had to attend new schools in unfamiliar locations. Initially, they were ostracized and often subjected to taunts. For years, Negro schools had been given hand-me-down textbooks that had been discarded by the white schools. White students knew this and would often write racial slurs and scribble offensive drawings and slogans in the books they turned in at the end of the year. Now young scholars were expected to share.

In May of 1956, two students at Florida A&M University decided to take a stand. Empowered by the story of Rosa Parks who had refused to give up her seat to a white man on an Alabama bus, Wilhelmina Jakes and Carrie Patterson seated themselves near the front of a Tallahassee bus. They refused the driver's order for them to move to the rear. When he ordered them off the bus entirely, they asked for their money back. He refused. The police were called; the girls were arrested. Two days later, FAMU student Brodes Hartley headed up a rally on campus and called for a boycott. The quiet Bethel Missionary Baptist Church minister Reverend Charles Kenzie Steele concluded that the time had come to take a decisive stand against segregation. A meeting was held at Bethel Church that drew hundreds of black clergy, independent business owners and folks that had just plain had enough. Steele formed the Inter-Civic Council (ICC) in order to fight back. Local attorney Thereis C. Lindsey provided legal advice to the group. The ICC helped to organize nonviolent protests, coordinated information in the community and acted as a powerful force in negotiations with government officials.

It was not the first time Reverend Steele had stepped forward to speak out for justice. He had always been a vocal supporter of civil rights initiatives. Family members report that Charles started preaching in his native West Virginia when he was just eight years old. He was ordained in the ministry when he was twenty-one. Reverend Steele had earned a degree from Morehouse College and had been married eleven years when he assumed the pastorship at Bethel in 1952. Though he was soft-spoken, his sermons were direct and inspirational. He almost always wore a suit and a bow tie and, like the good Father Hugon, he enjoyed an occasional "good" pipe. He never advocated violent action, but he was not a passive man either. Those who knew him said he was always calm, never showed fear and never raised his voice. During the protests of the 1950s, a cross was burned on Steele's front lawn, his life was threatened several times and "unknown persons" fired shots into his home that penetrated the inner walls. In the fall of 1956, over four hundred Ku Klux Klan (KKK) members dressed in their trademark white robes and hoods paraded past Steele's Bethel Church during a Sunday morning service. Reverend Steele was understandably concerned for the safety of his family, his congregation and for the community as a whole, but he repeatedly made public statements that he was "not afraid." His courage was contagious.

Students may have kicked off the bus boycott, but it was Reverend Steele and the ICC that organized it and kept it going. They set up carpools to transport people wherever they needed to go. Some sixty-five vehicle owners registered with the Inter-Civic Council, and the operation was supervised by Dan Speed. If you needed a ride, you called the ICC office and they made the necessary arrangements. In response, the city police department started arresting volunteer drivers and their passengers for operating public taxis without a license. Reverend Steele was among those who were charged. From the city's perspective, some of the vehicles being supplied by volunteers were less than safe, some drivers had inadequate insurance and the ICC was essentially operating a franchised "for hire" cab company without following regulations.

On occasion, someone would call for calm. A few prominent whites, like bank owner George Lewis and his wife, Clifton, stepped forward and took proactive stands against inequality. Fifty years after the bus boycott, the *Tallahassee Democrat* apologized for their civil rights news coverage and editorials. Patrick Dorsey, publisher, and Bob Gabordi, managing editor, issued a personal apology to Reverend Steele's family and a public one to the community in 2006. They noted that, while the paper condemned acts of violence and property destruction, they did not take a forceful stand against discriminatory practices. In a thoughtful article written at the same time, well-known and respected *Democrat* reporter Gerald Ensley observed, "On the whole, the *Democrat* covered the start of the Tallahassee civil rights movement with journalistic professionalism. Its editorial support took a little longer."

In August, two black drivers were hired to drive city buses on "Negro" routes, but that did not stop the boycott. By October, the city had taken the ICC and seven of its leaders to court for operating the alleged "for hire" cab venture. The municipal court ruled that they were doing just that, so the ICC stopped running the carpool. However, the boycott continued. That December the United States Supreme Court ruled that segregated seating on municipal transit in Montgomery, Alabama, was unconstitutional. On the twenty-second of that month, Reverend Steele announced that the boycott would end, but the next day the city announced it would continue its policy of segregated seating. The issue swung back and forth until a federal judge in Miami issued a ruling on January 3, 1957, that agreed with the Supreme Court. The city still voted to maintain segregated seating, but reversed itself on January 7, due to "legal concerns" about the policy.

In 1957 Reverend Steele joined with Dr. Martin Luther King Jr., Reverend Ralph Abernathy, Fred Shuttlesworth and others to form the Southern Christian Leadership Conference (SCLC). The group invited ministers from all over the South to an organizational meeting in Atlanta. The SCLC took much of their inspiration and energy from students like Carrie and Wilhelmina and other young people who participated in sit-ins, marches, boycotts and demonstrations all over the United States. Reverend Steele served as the organization's vice-president and participated in the famous Selma to Montgomery march.

Into the 1960s, local students continued to hold protest marches in front of downtown stores and movie theaters. Local civil rights leaders asked national associates to help. In February 1960, eleven clergymen—some white and some black—arrived from several other states and staged a sit-in at a local restaurant. They were arrested and subsequently set free after paying bonds of $1,000 each. At trial, eight of them were convicted and given sentences of sixty days in jail or a fine of $500 each. They elected not to pay the fine and their incarceration drew national attention. In a surprise move by local authorities, they were released not long afterward. Lunch counters at McCrory's, Walgreens and Sears were also targeted for their segregationist policies. On March 12, 23 African American students were arrested for sitting down at counters reserved for whites. That afternoon, over 250 student supporters marched in protest.

Gradually, local protests became less and less frequent and the national press looked to other cities for news. The people of Frenchtown were doing their best to attend to the more mundane challenges of daily life. The school integration process had begun. The buses were running as smoothly as possible and most of the boycotts were over.

A crowd gathered at the Leon County Courthouse to await the outcome of the trial of eleven civil rights demonstrators who were arrested in 1960. *Photo courtesy of the Florida State Archives Photo Collection.*

Discrimination was still a sad reality, but sweeping civil rights legislation at the national level seemed to offer some beacon of hope—that is, until Dr. Martin Luther King Jr. was assassinated on April 4, 1968.

In the days that followed, violence broke out in over one hundred cities in the United States Racial unrest was no longer focused on local issues. Shock and grief over the loss of such a dynamic and respected leader swept over the nation and the world. In Tallahassee, grief exploded into anger at the Florida A&M University campus. A relatively small group of students started throwing bottles and other projectiles at passing cars. At least one driver was seriously wounded by broken glass. The "protest" spread to a mobile home sales lot where two trailers were set on fire. Responding firemen were also pelted with anything that could be thrown. The police arrived but only succeeded in dispersing the crowd temporarily. The rioters moved up Adams Street, rolling barrels into moving traffic and throwing things at drivers who slowed to avoid hitting the obstacles. From there, the crowd turned up Wahnish Way. Sniper fire rang out from an unknown location on campus. Before nightfall, the police had managed to cordon off a four-block area. Police shot out streetlights to mask their position. More small-arms fire reportedly came from the campus and police responded with tear gas. Sometime during the night, an "unknown person, or persons" firebombed Crow's Grocery on Lake Bradford Road, resulting in the riot's only death. Ironically, the Crow family had operated one of the few white-owned businesses in that section of town that had welcomed black patrons for decades.

The following day, violence broke out in Frenchtown. The Home Furniture Store on North Monroe ignited when a firebomb was tossed through a rear window. The building's sprinkler system saved the structure but most of its contents were lost. Waldo's Furniture store on West Fourth burned completely. FAMU President Gore shut down the university and the dormitories were evacuated. Sheriff William Joyce ordered all liquor stores to close and most of the stores that sold ammunition refused to sell to anyone. Governor Claude Kirk as well as civic leaders called for calm. By Sunday morning, things had settled down. Reverend Raleigh N. Gooden of Frenchtown's St. Mary's Primitive Baptist Church organized memorial services in Dr. King's honor. Over four hundred people joined Reverend Gooden in a fifteen-block walk that led past the Capitol. Later, Reverend Gooden would say he organized the event to keep students "guided in the right direction."

There were times that segregationist beliefs manifested themselves in the cruelest ways. Lynchings, brutal beatings and fear of attack from organizations like the KKK could make life seem like one more stop on the road to Hades itself. Other times, prejudice and discrimination took on more subtle manifestations.

Alpha Omega Campbell was born in Quincy, Florida, in the summer of 1889. As a young man, he was given the opportunity to attend medical school in Boston and he eagerly accepted. He returned to Tallahassee and opened his first practice in Frenchtown in 1913. He built a beautiful home on Virginia Street, and over the years he amassed a considerable amount of property. People who remember him start out by saying he never turned away anyone who needed medical care. He treated both black and white alike, and whether you were rich, poor or in-between made no difference in the care you received. Dr. Campbell was identified as a mulatto in both the 1910 and 1920 Censuses. His wife was also mulatto, but was quite often mistaken for white. There were occasional murmurs of disapproval from those who assumed theirs was a "mixed" marriage, but the people who knew him never gave it a second thought. His reputation grew and it was not unusual for people to drive long distances to see him in preference to other physicians. In 1947 Dr. Campbell opened a pioneering, two-story, twenty-bed hospital and named it the Laura Bell Memorial Hospital in memory of his daughter, who had died at age twelve in 1931. The facility was one of the region's first privately owned hospitals that would treat Negro patients.

In the fall of 1955, Dr. Campbell's world started to crumble. He was accused of having performed illegal abortions—one of which allegedly resulted in the death of a twenty-one-year-old white female patient and mother of two small children. He was charged with manslaughter. Campbell admitted that he had treated the woman, but only to try to save her life after a doctor in a neighboring county had botched the original procedure. The black community rallied behind Dr. Campbell, as did a number of prominent white

The sign out front reads A&M Hotel in this 1966 photo. This building originally housed the Laura Bell Memorial Hospital and Campbell Clinic. When the facility was closed amid a great deal of public controversy, Frenchtown supporters "disguised" the building with the false name, though a few people did take up unauthorized occupancy for a short time. *Photo courtesy of Terry E. Lewis and the Florida State University Strozier Library.*

citizens. He was forced to sell off almost everything he had of value, including real estate holdings in two counties. The clinic was closed down. As his legal bills mounted, Frenchtown residents took up collections. The local lodge even took out a mortgage on their property. Over thirty witnesses were called during the trial, but the most damning testimony came from the woman's mother who swore that her daughter had told her Dr. Campbell was the only doctor she had seen. The all-white male jury would later claim the hearsay "deathbed" statement was the reason they voted for the physician's conviction. In the end, most observers agreed there was very little justice to be found in the Leon County Courthouse for the beloved physician. At the age of sixty-seven, Alpha Omega Campbell was sentenced to four years of hard labor at the notorious Florida State Prison at Starke. He lost his medical license and virtually everything he owned. The lodge lost their building and the Frenchtown community lost a trusted friend and an essential medical facility. Upon his release in 1959, Campbell and his family moved to Broward County, where he died on December 13, 1977.

Dr. Alpha Omega Campbell's home was one of the most beautiful residential structures in Frenchtown. It sat beside the clinic on Virginia Street. *Photo courtesy of Terry E. Lewis and the Florida State University Strozier Library.*

The Jim Crow era eventually dissolved in a series of legal rulings and new civil rights laws, and the resulting economic effects of desegregation were as dramatic as some of the social ones. The residents of Frenchtown were no longer restricted to patronizing only those stores and businesses located in their own neighborhood. The 1970s ushered in a new age of shopping malls, and transportation was more accessible than ever. One by one, Frenchtown businesses began to fail and no new businesses were moving in. The unemployment rate began to climb and urban blight took its place. Some houses were abandoned or allowed to deteriorate beyond anything that would have met the government's standard of "decent, safe, and sanitary." Empty buildings became havens for drug dealers and the homeless. The criminal element started to operate openly on street corners and in vacant lots. Residents no longer recognized all the passersby. Public housing suffered under the massive budget cuts of the second Reagan administration, and Frenchtown became known as the one place in town folks wanted to avoid after dark.

The 600 block of North Bronough was lined with fourteen simple, ill-equipped homes in this 1951 photo. They were occupied by twenty-three families who shared an outdoor, two-section toilet facility. *Photo courtesy of the Florida State Archives Photo Collection.*

By 1960, Frenchtown residents were patronizing stores and restaurants outside the community. Existing businesses gradually closed. This old store on West Brevard was representative of the neighborhood's downhill spiral toward urban blight. *Photo courtesy of the Florida State Archives Photo Collection.*

Reverend Charles Kenzie Steele became a national figure in the civil rights movement, but he never stopped serving the people of Frenchtown. When he passed away in 1980, he was still attending his flock at Bethel Church. Today, a statue of C.K. Steele is the focal point of the local bus system's main transfer terminal. The plaza that surrounds it was named in his honor.

Chapter 8

DEFINING FRENCHTOWN

I f there is one thing in town that eludes resolution, it is reaching an agreement on the geographic boundaries of Frenchtown. The original Northern Addition was roughly bound by Brevard on the north, Boulevard on the east (now MLK Boulevard), Park Avenue to the south and Dewey Street to the west, an area covering approximately twelve blocks. Historians will steadfastly argue that the Northern Addition and Frenchtown are one and the same. Those who grew up in sections of—or adjacent to—Frenchtown agree with the same north, east and west boundaries, but insist Frenchtown ended at Tennessee on the south, where the Springfield neighborhood stood between it and downtown. Outsiders who recall the era of urban blight and crime that plagued the area during the 1980s and '90s will tell you that Frenchtown stretched north all the way to Tharpe Street and as far as west as Woodward. They will concede that Tennessee and MLK form the outside limits to the east and west. Occasionally, someone will come along and claim that Frenchtown also included the black-owned businesses that once thrived along Monroe Street—some four blocks to the east of MLK Boulevard. Urban planners are more focused on funding than historical accuracy. Over the years, they have incorporated adjacent areas in order to pursue additional state, federal and historic preservation funding. Residents were not pleased to see the central core of the community diluted in this way. For a time, the boundaries were redefined to conform to the blocks laid out in the Northern Addition—sort of. Officials added in the Springfield, Goodbread and Griffin Heights communities to create a unified historic district, but everyone knows not all of those neighborhoods are *really* part of Frenchtown, and no one will swear that the whole issue isn't subject to more change sometime in the future.

In the end, Frenchtown cannot be defined in geographical terms, but by its nature and its influence on the city of Tallahassee as a whole.

Negro Activities

IN THE

Fla. Centennial Celebration

PAGEANT

Friday, Nov. 14, 8:15 P. M.

PARADE

Saturday, Nov. 15, 11:00 A. M.

PATRIOTIC ADDRESS

Saturday, Nov. 15, 3:30 P. M.

NEGRO MUSIC

BAND   ORCHESTRA   VOICES

PAGEANT: "THE SPIRIT OF FREEDOM." The story of a Climb-
ing race in Song and Pantomine.   A century's growth of a strug-
gling people depicted in a series of pictures, strikingly dramatic and
powerful in their simplicity. FRIDAY EVENING, NOVEMBER
14, 8:15 o'clock. OUT-DOOR THEATRE on the HUNT ESTATE,
The Home of the Tallahassee Girl.

GENERAL ADMISSION   -   25c

Watch for the other announcements

This poster—printed by the Florida A&M College Press—announced the upcoming Tallahassee
Centennial Celebration in 1924. By that time, many of the community's social and patriotic events were
segregated. *Image courtesy of the Florida State Archives Photo Collection.*

Even in the worst of times, there was always a presence in Frenchtown that could not be easily defined. It was a spirit that could not be watered down by government policies or substantially altered by court rulings. Frenchtown had a life of its own that ebbed and flowed like the nearby waters of the Gulf of Mexico. The community was held together by spiritual faith and shared tribulations. Until recently, there were no signs to indicate you were entering or leaving the neighborhood. There was no single style of architecture to indicate which streets were included and which ones weren't.

Besides, no matter what the boundaries were, or are, no matter how wonderful or grim things may have appeared, there were always celebrations.

When Althemese Pemberton (now Barnes) was growing up in Frenchtown, preparing for the celebration of Emancipation Day on May 20 was a very big deal indeed. Neighbors would spend hours preparing roasted, smoked and barbecued meats for all to share. Elaborate cakes, cookies, cobblers and pies were washed down with gallons of sweet tea and lemonade. Schools would be dismissed early and families would travel to the country to participate in special events. There was always music and dancing. The traditional "plaiting" of the May Pole would usually take place at this time, during which a large post would be installed where everyone could see it. Participants would playfully string colorful streamers in and around the pole until it was festively decorated all the way to the ground. Emancipation Day was also a time to remember the past. Schoolchildren often performed plays to reenact the reading of the Emancipation Proclamation to Tallahassee slaves. Sometimes folks would reserve some quiet moments to walk down to the City Cemetery and place memorials on the graves of the black Union soldiers buried there.

The celebration of May Day was another huge event. Every school would schedule something special to mark the arrival of the special spring day. It was the time of year when nearly every girl in the community would get a new dress, each one hoping hers was the prettiest of all. One of the most elaborate festivals took place at Lincoln High School. Young ladies representing several different age groups would compete for the title of May Queen. The winner was allowed to preside over various and sundry events. A May Day evening event was held when the queen would be escorted down the aisle to the stage at the auditorium. She would be joined by her court, and the girls would be serenaded and heralded for their beauty and for having been elected by the student body to reign over the festivities. Each class wore special costumes and performed for the assembled crowds. Families, churches and the entire community would participate. Even today, a smile crosses Mrs. Barnes's face as she recalls how Emancipation Day and May Day seemed to be the most carefree days of the year.

Some say Frenchtown was at its finest in the days when there was a restaurant on every corner and a wide choice of nightclubs where patrons were treated to performances by some of the nation's best entertainers. New York had Harlem and Tallahassee had Frenchtown. Louis Armstrong came to town. Over the years, performers from Little Milton to Little Richard—including Cab Calloway, Al Green and Ray Charles—entertained enthusiastic crowds. Lou Rawls crooned more than one tune. Tallahassee

This building, located at the corner of Macomb and Virginia Streets, was built as the Knights of Pythias Hall. It was later transformed into the popular Red Bird Café. Many well-known African American entertainers performed at the Red Bird, including Ray Charles, Little Richard and Tallahassee residents Cannonball Adderley and his brother Nat. The building was torn down in 1970. *Photo courtesy of Terry E. Lewis and the Florida State University Strozier Library.*

was "on the road" between New Orleans and larger Florida cities and it was not unusual for entertainers to make a rest stop in Frenchtown and put on a show in the bargain. Folks did not always have to wait for music to come to them; there was plenty of local talent that went on to play in larger cities. Cannonball Adderley and his brother Nat came to Tallahassee to go to school. Their mother came with them, and the family settled into a small but comfortable home in Smokey Hollow. Frenchtown, however, was where they came to play. They frequently performed at the old Red Bird Café and other nightspots or would start up an impromptu jam session just about anywhere else folks would gather. Contemporary musician Michael Koppy recalls spending long afternoons in front of Ashmore's Drug Store just playing his guitar. One day, he met Emmett Goodman, who claimed to have just arrived in Frenchtown after having walked five hundred miles from Miami. He taught Michael how to change chords and lyrics to suit the mood and the moment—something most of the rhythm and blues performers of Frenchtown did with practiced ease.

90

This photo of Frenchtown's Macomb Street commercial district was taken in 1966. The E&K Clothing Store advertised merchandise "for the entire family." Crump's Tavern and Package Liquor Store was located a few doors down the street. *Photo courtesy of Terry E. Lewis and the Florida State University Strozier Library.*

There was plenty of gospel music pouring forth from every church. More than one entertainer belted out a solo with the church choir long before they stood on a nightclub stage. The seven original members of the Harmony Gales all claimed they traced their singing roots to the church. The group included Leroy "Jolly" Burgess, Al Cloves, Seth Gaines, Fred Robinson, Wesley and Willie Simmons and Isaiah Waymon. In a feature article written for the apostleofgod.com website in 2002, Burgess was asked why he thought they were still performing after more than fifty years. "Some lights are gone out, some wheels may be wobblin', bunch of us are bald-headed with a sense of humor, but we're still rollin' along," he laughed. And the music still pours forth from all those churches.

It wasn't just entertainers who stopped in to meet and greet the people of Frenchtown. Senator Julian Bond was a visitor. Author James Baldwin read some of his work to the students at FAMU and stayed overnight at the Tookes Hotel. During the Jim Crow years, African Americans were prohibited from staying in "whites only" hotels. James Tookes purchased a one-story frame house in Frenchtown in 1914 for $700. At the time,

In 1966, you could get old-fashioned barbecue at Minor's and also take home some fresh fish. This string of eight stores has recently been remodeled and still houses at least one restaurant. *Photo courtesy of Terry E. Lewis and the Florida State University Strozier Library.*

he was employed as a chef at the governor's mansion. In 1930, he married teacher Dorothy Nash. Back in the late 1880s, blacks could stay at the old Boulevard Hotel, but in the early 1950s, there was a pressing need for lodging. The Tookeses added three bedrooms and an extra bath to their home and opened a boardinghouse. They added more rooms in 1971 and continued to operate as a hotel into the 1980s. Over the years, the Tookes Hotel was also the site of wedding receptions and other celebrations. It was the first building in Frenchtown to be listed on the National Register of Historic Places. It is being extensively restored and there are plans to turn the property into a museum.

In 1949 gold medalist Jesse Owens came to town. Even though he had endeared himself to the American public for his spectacular performance at the 1936 Olympics, there was no place for him to stay in Tallahassee at the time. Dr. Campbell invited Owens to stay at his home. The next morning, much to the delight of the nurses at the Laura Bell Clinic, Jesse went next door to sign autographs and pose for pictures.

Sporting events were always a big part of Frenchtown life. Reatharia Davis moved to Frenchtown from the country with her mother and two sisters when she was in the third grade. Her mother worked all day at a college sorority house doing the cleaning and some of the cooking. Recently, Mrs. Davis shared her memories of what she would do on a typical school day: "I was the oldest, so I'd make the beds up and fix breakfast

Mr. Hadley and his sons operated one of the many grocery stores located in Frenchtown. In 1966 they advertised sirloin steak for eighty-nine cents per pound. *Photo courtesy of Terry E. Lewis and the Florida State University Strozier Library.*

so Momma could go to work. We had our chores to do, but I liked doing them early. When I got out of school, the first thing we would do was go over to the playground over near Macomb and watch the sports. There were swings to play on, but we wanted to watch the sports." Kids played games in the streets and also found areas to play baseball, basketball, football and kickball. The biggest treat of all was going over to the stadium to watch the teams of Florida A&M University.

In Tallahassee's early days, blacks and whites attended the same theaters and enjoyed the same traveling pony shows and circuses. During the Jim Crow years, blacks were shut out of most theaters. In 1930 Maggie Yellowhair opened the first movie house in Frenchtown. When her Capital Theatre opened, tickets only cost five cents. Ten years later, the Leon Theatre opened on Tennessee Street. It was a much larger building with seating for three hundred and had a stage that accommodated live performances. It was also a more expensive place to go. Kids and adults could still see movies at the Capital and tickets had only risen to seventy-five cents. In the 1980s the Capital was long since gone and the Leon had degraded to showing only X-rated adult films. The building was purchased in 1985 and the theater was shut down.

Bessie Hardin—"Miss Bessie" to all who love and adore her—recently took some of her friends and neighbors on a "memory tour" and she recalled her daily walks from Lincoln

Guests at Janice McCloud's 1940s birthday party included Ann, Carol and Barrie Roberts; the Mannings sisters; Howard Jackson; Ricky Pope; Carmen and Sonja Howell; Ralph and Francis Allen; Gloria Gilliam; and Peggy McGhee. Also attending were Joyce, Myra and Gloria Smith; Johnella Reid; Sandra and Gerald Cooper; and Josie Weaver. *Photo courtesy of the John G. Riley Center/Museum of African American History & Culture.*

School to her Frenchtown home back in the 1940s. "Right across the street from Lincoln, there was a lady who sold sandwiches and hamburgers, things like that. Her name was Miss Betty. Of course, that was in the days before you had to get all kinds of permits to sell food. She had a little building next to her house, but I guess she made most of those sandwiches in her own kitchen." Miss Bessie continued, "I can picture the whole walk home. Turning south from Lincoln, you would pass the Chicken Shack, then John Harper's Pool Room. Mr. Nims had a pool room and there was another one called Nell's Pool Room." As Mrs. Hardin continued her nostalgic walk back home, she named the businesses she would pass or see down the side streets: Frenchtown Cleaners, the E&K Clothing Store, Lloyd White's Barber Shop, Tampa's Store and a grocery or two. Miss Bessie smiled and added, "If you, or one of your friends, had some extra change, you'd go on over to Mr. Ashmore's store. He had ice cream cones that only cost a nickel."

Asked if she was afraid to walk past all those pool halls, Miss Bessie shook her head emphatically and replied, "No! Folks weren't afraid to walk the streets." On the contrary,

Edith Reid West, daughter of Cyrus and Mattie Reid, married Earl Henry West of New Jersey. They raised their children on West Georgia Street in Frenchtown. *Photo courtesy of the John G. Riley Center/Museum of African American History & Culture.*

each person you met knew who you were and knew your family. Each adult was another set of eyes to make sure you went where you were supposed to and didn't go where you weren't. If you got into mischief, your mother was likely to know about it long before you reached your front porch.

Families have always been important in Frenchtown. Names might be recorded in a family bible, but more often than not, relationships were locked in to the oral history of the community. Families were identified through cousins, aunts, uncles and grandparents. There was a time when a "newcomer" was anyone that hadn't been born in the town. Well into the twentieth century, families identified with ties to the black communities that formed in Leon County around the old plantations. Folks were from St. Peter's, Kirksey, Iamonia, China Hill and dozens of others. If you had been born in Frenchtown, you most likely had familial ties to others in outlying places. Sunday afternoon drives to the "old places" were a major treat.

Sunday mornings were also special. Most folks went to church. If you did not belong to Bethel Baptist, you went to St. Mary's Primitive Baptist Church or one of a dozen

Lee's Grocery faced Tennessee Street at the southernmost edge of Frenchtown. Today, this street is one of the busiest in Tallahassee. *Photo courtesy of the Florida State Archives Photo Collection.*

other churches that sit in and around Frenchtown. A 1930 map prepared by the Sanborn Insurance Company on behalf of the city recorded some of the amenities of each. The Triumph Sanctified Holiness Church on West Virginia Street had "stove heat" but no electricity. St. Mary's had both. The Pentecostal Holiness Church on North Bronough had no lights. The Sanborn Company surveyor made a note that Bethel was "large." If you did not go to services, someone would more than likely stop by your house to check if you were OK or just taking some well-deserved rest time.

Sunday was a day when dinner was a bit more extraordinary than others. Most everyone shopped early in the week to assure they could make the best selections. There were plenty of groceries to choose from. In 1934 the City Directory listed twenty-six businesses in Frenchtown and twelve of them were grocery stores. Proprietors included C. Goodman, T. Hadley, F. Johnson, W Woodberry, J. Wilson and J. Nims. Joe Nims was a fixture in Frenchtown for decades. *Tallahassee Democrat* staff writer Mike Abrams wrote a feature article about him when Mr. Nims was ninety-three years old and, in Nims's words, "Not about to die." Nims's Grocery was once one of the most popular stores in the area, but by 1976 Joe carried very little stock and the shelves were dusty. He recalled that he used to sell more meat than anything else. He related that his father raised cattle

96

The Tallahassee Curb Market operated near the corner of Gaines and Bloxham, but many of its vendors and patrons lived in Frenchtown. *Photo courtesy of the Florida State Archives Photo Collection.*

Florida A&M President Dr. Benjamin Perry (second from left) is pictured riding on a Springtime
Tallahassee float in 1970. The two men beside him are unidentified. Fred Barnes is driving the wagon.
Photo courtesy of the Florida State Archives Photo Collection.

and supplied meat to Frenchtown before the grocery opened. Joe used to make deliveries
by horse and wagon. "It was the custom," Joe recalled "to have meat for a big Sunday
dinner. People would take the meat, put it on a rope, and lower it into their wells to keep
it cool. Sunday, they'd bring it up."

Edna Dowd was born in rural Leon County, but her family moved into Frenchtown
when she was nine years old. She remembers her mother's shopping expeditions. "She
wore this long apron. She would walk on down to the store, get what she needed,
bundle it all up in that apron and walk on back home." She wondered why the apron
didn't split in half on some trips. Years later when the Star Market opened, everyone
flocked over there. It was newer, bigger and carried a wider selection. There are no such
establishments in Frenchtown today. There is a convenience store, but most everyone
heads out to Publix, Albertsons or the nearest Wal-Mart to get whatever they need.

If you didn't want to cook and you had the resources, there were plenty of restaurants
to choose from. E. Ford's Restaurant appeared in the 1914 City Directory. It was located
on West Virginia Street, but it seems to have gone out of business fairly quickly. On the

other hand, Ferrell's Restaurant has been operating off and on at the same location for over forty years. By all accounts, the Chicken Shack was *the* place to go for the best fried chicken in town. There were also places to get barbeque and places to get fish. There were restaurants open for breakfast and restaurants open for dinner and of course you could always stop by Miss Betty's to get a great burger.

Chapter 9

BRIGHT FUTURE ROOTED IN THE PAST

Frenchtown is strategically located to be a desirable residential and commercial area, but the cultural heritage of the neighborhood is very strong and it has successfully resisted much of the tear-it-down and build-something-new development that has consumed much of Tallahassee's downtown. Current gentrification is a remarkable study of how municipalities can promote progress while retaining heritage. Many locals consider the Renaissance Center on Macomb Street to be the symbol of Frenchtown's efforts at revitalization. It was conceived in 1998 by community leaders who wanted to replace abandoned and dilapidated properties with a facility that would improve the economic viability of the area. The "Ren" Center was developed by the McGinnis Booth Trust and the Frenchtown Community Development Corporation. Barnett Fronczak Architects designed the structure to mirror the historic early twentieth-century flavor of surrounding areas. A significant architectural feature is the clock tower that anchors the three-story building's corner. Culpepper Construction completed the building in April of 2005. The facility contains seventy thousand square feet of space and is served by an adjacent three-hundred-space parking garage. In 2006 the building was purchased under a joint venture initiative by the City of Tallahassee and Leon County. Today, it houses numerous city offices, including several divisions of utility services where residents can set up a new account or pay an existing bill. Business owners can apply for occupational licenses there and taxi drivers can secure permits. Several organizations and civic-minded groups use the building's available meeting space.

This photo was taken in 1948. Sullivan's Food Store is seen to the left. Ashmore's Drug Store had moved into the building next door—which once housed Ransom Upholstery—and had just installed one of the community's first neon signs. *Photo courtesy of the Florida State Archives Photo Collection.*

If the Renaissance Center is one of Frenchtown's primary symbols of the future, then surely the preservation of Ashmore's Drug Store stands as an example of honoring the past. Everyone seems to know where the store is. Ask a local for directions and they are likely to give them in relation to Ashmore's shop on West Brevard. Rob Roy Ashmore bought the Frenchtown property back in 1945 just after he returned from duty as an army medical corpsman. Originally, it was a drugstore of sorts. Ashmore's never had a pharmacist and did not fill prescriptions. It did, however, sell Red Rooster Pills, which were practically guaranteed to help anyone gain or maintain vitality. If you didn't think that would do the trick, he kept plenty of cod liver oil and Geritol in stock. Mr. Ashmore also had a soda fountain that Frenchtown children visited as often as possible. On a recent summer's afternoon, during a visit with the Bethel Towers Apartments' After Lunch Bunch, several long-term residents of Frenchtown recalled that Mr. Ashmore served the coldest Coca-Colas in town at his soda fountain. They only cost a nickel back then, and kids couldn't wait to get out of school and run down there and get one. What's more, whether you had any money or not, Mr. Ashmore never chased anyone away as long as they were behaving. More recently, Ashmore operated his business as a combination used furniture and antique store, but he also had an odd collection of miscellaneous stuff that almost defied description. Ashmore sold the business—including many of its contents—to the city in 2004, and there are plans to turn it into a permanent museum. A lot of people think Mr. Ashmore should stay on as its director. No one would argue that he probably knows as much about the history of Frenchtown as anyone and he is a consummate storyteller. If you go into the store looking for a particular item, you may very well find it, but you are just as likely to be treated to a tale of how he came to be in possession of it in the first place, as well as hear a treatise on why it was ever invented. Before long, a previously uninitiated shopper will be overcome with reverence for the artifact. Ashmore will finally announce the item is "not for sale" and the shopper will end up walking out of the store without it. Over the years, Ashmore has played host to a wide variety of shoppers and curious visitors. A 2004 *Tallahassee Democrat* article quoted Rob Roy as saying, "I've met royalty to the homeless on the street at my little shop, and they're all the same to me." He is right. Everyone is—and has always been—welcomed at Ashmore's.

Ashmore's did not fill prescriptions, but the Economy Drug Store did—and still does today. Original owner Howard Roberts was a registered pharmacist of considerable note. Back in the days when FAMU was setting up its prestigious School of Pharmacy, Roberts assisted Dr. L.H.B. Foote in the endeavor. Mr. Roberts was a native of Sanford, Florida, and held degrees from both Florida A&M and Howard Universities. When Dr. Foote invited Roberts to Tallahassee, there were no "black" drugstores in Leon County. Howard seized the opportunity to help his old professor and fill a critical gap in services. He settled in Frenchtown and went to work. Roberts's daughter, Alexis McMillan, followed in his footsteps. She is a registered pharmacist and has been running her dad's business since his death in

Ashmore's Drug Store was a popular place to stop in for a cold soda or an over-the-counter product that was sure to cure almost anything. It has been a Frenchtown landmark for many years. Today, it offers an eclectic selection of antiques. Plans are being made to convert the property into a permanent museum of local memorabilia. *Photo by J. Hare.*

1990. Mom Geraldine is a druggist too and also a professor at FAMU. The Roberts family has always worked together—and on behalf of the Frenchtown community. They are chronic volunteers and Frenchtown is glad there is no pill to cure that.

The Bethel Missionary Baptist Church has grown beyond anything Reverend James Page might have imagined back in 1870. Bethel has provided strong leadership and wise council to the residents of Frenchtown through the uncertain days of Reconstruction, the trying times of Jim Crow, the turbulent trials of the civil rights struggle and countless attempts to improve and revitalize the physical surroundings of the community. Over the years, many men and women have been a part of those efforts, and all of them have left legacies of amazing service.

The Reverend Horace Bailey assumed leadership after James Page died in 1883. Reverend Bailey served until 1899. J.B. Hankerson took over in 1900 and served for eighteen years. A.L. Pettus, C.L. Stamps and J.P. West shared the ministry over the years 1918 to 1928. Pastors who followed included Harry Jones (1928–1930), Jerome

Harris (1930–1931) and William Burns (1931–1951). Dr. Charles Kenzie Steele Sr. assumed the role of pastor in 1952 and served in that capacity until 1980. He was followed by his friend and associate, Herbert Alexander (1981–1985).

Each of them helped the church grow and was there for the Bethel congregation in both good times and bad, but perhaps no one played a more dramatic role in changing the face of Frenchtown than Dr. R.B. Holmes.

Reverend Holmes is quick to smile and has an easygoing manner about him that sets people immediately at ease. There is, however, no doubt about the firm resolve hidden in his expression. He is a well-educated man who holds various degrees from Central Florida Junior College, Malone College in Ohio, Methodist Theological Seminary in Delaware and Virginia Union University. Holmes came to Tallahassee from Jacksonville, Florida, in 1986 and went to work without delay.

First and foremost, Bethel members would tell you that Reverend Holmes is a minister of the Gospel, but he is also a teacher and a man of vision when it comes to providing services to the community. Over his years of service, Bethel Church has purchased several buildings and properties in, and adjacent to, Frenchtown. They have repurposed some structures, built new ones and expanded services to the community.

Within a year of assuming the Bethel leadership post, Holmes instituted a summer camp program that was named in C.K. Steele's honor. The Bethel Christian Academy was opened in 1992 for boys and girls from pre-kindergarten to third grade. The C.K. Steele-LeRoy Collins Community Charter School opened in 1996. The facility was the county's first charter school and is open to all students in grades six to eight. The school offers all required state courses and is fully accredited. Steele-Collins students have consistently scored well on state exams, have been cited for high achievement in several areas and participate in the International Baccalaureate Program.

The Bethel Family Restaurant was one of Reverend Holmes's most creative ventures. The full-service restaurant and catering facility provides good food and fellowship in a family atmosphere. In addition, they are able to handle food services for the schools and other community events. The bold move created new jobs and rekindled Frenchtown's entrepreneurial spirit.

Meeting spiritual, educational and economic needs was just the beginning of Reverend Holmes's work. In 1998, construction began on the multimillion-dollar Bethel Family Life Center. The 36,000-square-foot, two-story building houses a computer lab, a gymnasium, community meeting rooms and other facilities designed to meet social and recreational needs. There are also classrooms for adult education and a multitude of social programs. It is also the new home of the ever-growing Bethel Christian Academy. The center opened in 1999.

The Bethel Family Counseling and Outreach Center and the associated Bethel Mental Health Center opened in 2002. The facility is staffed with a psychiatrist, licensed clinicians and masters-level therapists who take a holistic approach toward treating mental and emotional disorders. The clinic provides a wide range

The Bethel Family Life Center is a Frenchtown showpiece and offers a multitude of faith-based, social and educational services and other family activities. *Photo by J. Hare.*

The Carter-Howell-Strong Park offers green space and a pond that helps to control age-old drainage problems in Frenchtown. *Photo by J. Hare.*

of counseling services as well as medication management and other ongoing treatment programs.

Bethel Missionary Church has also played an important role in the development of affordable housing. Bethel Towers Apartments opened in 2002. The $5-million facility provides fifty-nine single-bedroom, single-bath units for income-restricted seniors over the age of sixty-two. Residents can secure hot meals in the central dining room, have access to on-site laundry facilities and can participate in a multitude of social activities. Bethel buses are available for trips to local stores, doctor's appointments and special field trips. The Carolina Oaks Development is Bethel's latest venture in the housing industry. Once again, Reverend Holmes supplied the vision for a neighborhood of single-family homes. He helped create Housing Tallahassee, a limited liability corporation that is a shining example of creative partnering among government, a faith-based organization and the private sector. The site selected for Carolina Oaks was once home to Carolina Place—a run-down, crime-infested apartment complex that was eventually demolished by the city. The land was secured at a cost of $2.8 million and the city provided a zero percent, $750,000 loan to help finance construction. Additional public funding was later provided to build sidewalks and offset infrastructure costs. St. Joe Towns and Resorts represented the development end of the partnership. Builders, such as Aspirant Homes of Tallahassee, coordinated design plans that created a 1930s, Charleston-like ambiance that tied the development to the surrounding neighborhood architecturally. The homes are priced below market, and low-interest, low down-payment loans backed by state-supplied housing dollars were made available through firms like BB&T Mortgage Company. A groundbreaking ceremony took place in October of 2005 and already new homeowners have moved in.

Bethel Missionary Baptist Church started with just under two hundred members. Today, the congregation is numbered in the thousands. It continues to meet the spiritual needs of the Frenchtown community and beyond in the same way that Reverend James Page did so many years ago.

Minor flooding and storm water drainage problems have plagued Frenchtown for many years. Low-lying areas receive runoff from hills to the north and excessive construction to its south forces water back into the community. Generations of Frenchtown residents have complained about the situation. In 1987 the Frenchtown Drainage Project was created as a partnership that included the Frenchtown Neighborhood Improvement Association, local residents and the City of Tallahassee. Engineers from the Department of Public Works felt the problems could be corrected by building a holding pond near the center of the community. The result of their labor was the Carter-Howell-Strong Park, which was dedicated on February 10, 1993. Its name honors the many contributions of some exceptional people who grew up in Frenchtown and whose influence spread throughout Leon County.

Aquilina Casanas Howell grew up on Georgia Street. Her love of learning led her to become a teacher. She later served as a key administrator in the Leon County School System. The district's Instructional Service Center was named in her honor.

The Ash Gallery is owned and operated by Annie Roberts Harris. Harris is a driving force behind Frenchtown revitalization. *Photo by J. Hare.*

When Mrs. Howell retired, she continued to volunteer her time for the benefit of various community and civic organizations. She was among the first to suggest that a park should be built around the holding pond. She urged city administrators and commissioners to allocate additional funding to add special plantings, sidewalks and benches, and they agreed. Before long, the Tallahassee Parks and Recreation Department and the police department were brought into the partnership and plans for building a community park around the holding pond were finalized.

Eunice Spence Carter grew up on the corner of Copeland and Virginia Streets. When the park was built, her home was on one of the forty-five parcels that had to be cleared for construction. Her personal sacrifice was no surprise to those who knew her. She frequently put the needs of others above her own. Mrs. Carter was an educator and spent much of her career teaching at Lincoln High School. Former students remember her as demanding, but always willing to take the time to offer additional help. The beloved teacher passed away in 1992.

The Strong-Jones Funeral Home has been doing business in Frenchtown for decades. Thomas Strong purchased the Mitchell Funeral Home on West Carolina Street in the 1940s. Elbert W. Jones assisted him in providing burial services to

The Frenchtown Community Development Center (CDC) purchased and rehabilitated this small bungalow for their busy office. It is located adjacent to the new Carolina Oaks development. *Photo by J. Hare.*

Leon County's African American community. When Thomas died in 1947, Jones purchased a half-interest in the business, became the new funeral director and formed the Strong-Jones partnership with Mamie Johnson Strong and her son Robert. Mamie supported her neighbors during times of grief and during times of need. Both mother and son were active volunteers and assumed leadership roles in the community. The funeral home continues to operate under the direction of Mamie's grandson, Darrell Lawrence, and Mr. Jones's daughter, Linn Ann Griffin.

An article that appeared in the *Tallahassee Democrat* on March 1, 2005, pointed out that Frenchtown was being revitalized one step at a time, "then Annie Harris jumped in, and took three steps." Back in the 1960s, Ann moved to Tallahassee from Alabama to attend Florida A&M University. Her career took her to central Florida for some time, but she returned in 1998 and was startled to see how much Frenchtown had deteriorated during her absence. She remembered the days when neighbors all knew each other and businesses were still local. Her move was the city's gain. She went back to work for the Leon County School District where she had spent most of the '70s and '80s as a teacher. Harris retired as the assistant superintendent of teaching and learning. Being a leader is second nature for Ann, who has always been an enthusiastic community-service volunteer. When she retired, she was not ready to put those skills out to pasture. She purchased three homes in Frenchtown and turned each one of them into a business. The Ash Gallery is one of them. The small specialty shop carries an eclectic mix of artwork, jewelry and fashion accessories. One of her properties is used as a meeting place for small groups; the third is currently rented out as a private residence. It was once the home of the late civil rights activist, Mary Ola Gaines. The historic property may have fallen to the wrecking ball if it had not been rescued by Mrs. Harris. She invested large sums of money and a lot of hours to remodel and rehabilitate all three homes. She did not stop there. In 2006, Ann Harris and her husband, Early, moved into their brand new home in the Carolina Oaks Development.

There is only one thing that makes it difficult to talk about Frenchtown revitalization and that is trying to keep track of all the players. The secret to making plans work seems to be in forming effective partnerships, and there are plenty of folks interested in doing just that. The first efforts to eliminate urban blight conditions started back in 1973 when the Frenchtown Merchant's Association was formed by pharmacist and Economy Drug Store owner H.A. Roberts and other businessmen in the area. Roberts was disappointed in the group's initial activities. They ended up sponsoring events and activities rather than getting down to the business of renovating buildings and improving transportation, but Mr. Roberts never gave up on his dream to reenergize Frenchtown. The City of Tallahassee did not step forward until 1985, when the commission reviewed a report that painted a bleak picture of Frenchtown conditions. That same week, Tallahassee police raided Perry's Disco and another nightclub and arrested sixty people under a "disorderly house" law that was subsequently ruled unconstitutional. While the city considered a revitalization plan funded with almost $1 million, most of it was earmarked for demolition. One city official suggested that, "In order to change the social character of the area, you have to eliminate some of the things on the Macomb Street corridor." He may have been right, but at the time Frenchtown residents were not convinced. The city commission delayed any action.

The Frenchtown Area Development Authority was organized in 1982. The group envisioned transforming Frenchtown into a mini-French Quarter, and the city provided $450,000 in federal money to help them do it. Later, they were criticized for not spending the money wisely. Over half of the funds were spent on administrative costs.

By 1988 crime was rampant in Frenchtown. Drugs were being sold in broad daylight and Frenchtown residents were just plain scared about the direction the neighborhood was going. In a May 1988 article written by Kathleen Laufenburg for the *Tallahassee Democrat*, Rosa Lee Thomas was quoted as saying, "It's the devil around here. You can't even sleep at night. I hear guns going off out here...I used to be able to go out there and pick up pecans, and have a garden. But now, I can't even leave a light bulb on—they steal the bulb!" Police organized several sweeps of the area in hopes of taking control. One of the areas they targeted was referred to as "Hang Out Hole"—a wooded area behind the storefront properties of Macomb Street. Rosa Thomas witnessed several arrests and cheered the officers on.

In 1992 Frenchtown leaders worked with the Bureau of Historic Preservation in Tallahassee and managed to secure a $60,000 grant from the National Trust. The plan was to repair thirty historic homes in Frenchtown that the local bureau had identified and documented and then sell them to qualifying low-income families. The Housing Development Corporation of Tallahassee partnered in the initiative. Potential homeowners received counseling in the responsibilities of homeownership and, for the most part, the plan worked.

There were numerous organizations that helped in the early efforts to return Frenchtown to a neighborhood where existing residents felt safe and new people and businesses wanted to move in. The now-defunct Tallahassee Housing Foundation made home repairs and offered energy-saving retrofits that were primarily funded with state money and private donations. Volunteers with Habitat for Humanity repaired some homes and built new ones. Operation Commitment brought city work crews in to prune trees, clean gutters, replace street signs and fix broken lights. The police department set up bike patrols, and officers took time out to get to know residents and let residents get to know them. Federal and state grants were awarded, local banks provided loans and Leon County government kicked in huge sums of money.

Some efforts were more successful than others. Some—like a recent proposal to tear down more structures to make way for another storm-water holding pond—have been controversial. Through it all, one thing is clear: Frenchtown is on its way back, and it still has some key players that are determined to finally get the job done.

The Tallahassee chapter of the Urban League was established in 1969. Charter members included Dr. Benjamin Perry, president of Florida A&M University, Alice

Peacock and Ed Dussie. The organization originally occupied a building owned by James Tookes. When they needed more room, they moved their operations to a Brevard Street location. In 1976 the Urban League purchased an abandoned nightclub on Old Bainbridge. Since then, the building has been altered, repaired and expanded and today houses a full-time staff of fourteen. Repairing existing properties has always been an important part of what the Urban League does. Over the years, the league has replaced roofs, painted exteriors and made hundreds of modifications that have improved security, accessibility and energy efficiency. The Urban League has also built some in-fill housing in Frenchtown and holds frequent homebuyer seminars to help people all over town to make the leap from renter to homeowner. Educational programs are not limited to housing; they also offer classes in pregnancy prevention and male responsibility. Their victim support program provides critical assistance and counseling to victims of crime, including home invasion robberies, assaults, domestic violence and rape. The Urban League also supports local recreational centers, matches tutors with students who need additional help and provides job-seeking assistance. In short, the league acts as a primary provider of non-public social services that make a difference at the grassroots level. Local promotions for the Urban League feature the phrase "We're making a difference," and they have been doing it for over thirty-five years under the direction of the same leader, President Ernest Ferrell.

The signs of a revitalized Frenchtown are popping up all over the neighborhood. Each new park, building, community center, house and monument represents a small piece of history, and the hundreds of people who have shared their vision of a place where both residents and visitors feel at home. Perhaps there is no better symbol of the individual paths Frenchtown supporters have taken to lead us to common ground than the tiny F.D. Lee Park that sits at the corner of Carolina and Macomb Streets.

Frederick Douglass Lee Sr. was the first African American hired to serve on Tallahassee's police force. In 1952 Lee was working as a chef at Leon High School. The city was making a concerted effort to integrate its force, and local civil rights activists encouraged him to apply. He was assigned to patrol the Frenchtown community and he accomplished that task under very difficult circumstances. In the beginning, he had no patrol car; he walked. Later, he was given a three-wheeled motorcycle and finally a regulation police vehicle. In the early years of his service, if he had to make an arrest, he was required to call in a white officer to take charge of the offender. In an article that appeared in the *Capital Outlook*, Lee's son, Darryl, recalled that his father "would sometimes see some of the Frenchtown folk at the local bar. There were times my father called a cab for a drunk neighbor rather than turn him in…and he paid the cab fare too." Lee was a large and imposing individual and very few people were willing to test his patience—or his physical strength. He could be thoughtful and kind but firm and resolute as well. He rose to the rank of sergeant and retired in 1972. Lee passed away one year later. A park was later dedicated in his honor near the central area of Frenchtown. The ceremony was

This monument, and the surrounding park area, was built to honor the memory of Officer Frederick Douglass Lee. His likeness stands between two children. *Photo by J. Hare.*

attended by friends and family, public dignitaries and residents who remembered that he was fair and always took the time to listen to what they had to say. The main feature of the park is a three-figure sculpture created by the well-known artist Chester L. Williams. Officer Lee is standing between two small children. To the casual observer, he appears to be softly chiding a little boy to return his sister's doll to her outstretched arms. It is a fitting tribute to a man who was known as an exceptional mediator and who always took the time to stop and talk with the littlest of Frenchtown's residents.

BIBLIOGRAPHY

Barnes, Althemese, and Debra Herman. *African-American Education in Leon County, Florida: Emancipation Through Desegregation 1863–1968*. Tallahassee: The John G. Riley Center/ Museum of African-American History & Culture, 2001.

Barnes, Althemese, and Ann Roberts. *Tallahassee, Florida: Black America Series*. Charleston, SC: Arcadia Press, 2000.

Brueckheimer, Dr. William R., Sara Hay Lamb, and Gwendolyn B. Waldorf. *Rural Resources of Leon County, Florida 1821–1950*. Vol. 1. Tallahassee: Historic Contexts and Case Studies, Historic Tallahassee Preservation Board, 1992.

Coles, David J. "'Hell By the Sea': Florida's Camp Gordon Johnston in World War II." *The Florida Historical Quarterly* 73, no. 1 (July 1994).

Davidson, Alvie L. *Florida Land Records*. Bowie, MD: Heritage Books, 1989.

Davis, Ronald L.F. "Creating Jim Crow: In-Depth Essay." *The History of Jim Crow*. New York Life. http://www.jimcrowhistory.org/home.htm

Ellis, Mary Louise, and William Warren Rogers. *Tallahassee and Leon County: A History and Bibliography*. Tallahassee: Florida Department of State, 1986.

———. Joan Perry Morris, photo ed. *Tallahassee: Favored Land—A History of Tallahassee and Leon County*. Tallahassee: The Donning Company Publishers for the Tallahassee Trust for Historic Preservation, 1988.

Bibliography

Ensley, Gerald. *Tallahassee Democrat: 100 Years*. Tallahassee: The Tallahassee Democrat, 2005.

Gannon, Michael. *The New History of Florida*. Gainesville: University Press of Florida, 1996.

Groene, Bertram H. *Ante-Bellum Tallahassee*. Tallahassee: Florida Heritage Foundation, 1971.

Guzman, William, and Tameka Bradley Hobbs. *Landmarks and Legacies: A Guide to Tallahassee's African-American Heritage 1865–1970*. Tallahassee: The John G. Riley Center/Museum of African-American History & Culture, 2000.

Hanna, A.J. *A Prince In Their Midst: The Adventurous Life of Achille Murat On The American Frontier*. Norman: University of Oklahoma Press, 1946.

Hobbs, Willie. "The King of Love." PhD diss., Florida State University, 2006.

Howard, Walter T. "Vigilante Justice and National Reaction: The 1937 Tallahassee Double Lynching." *The Florida Historical Quarterly* 67, no. 1 (July 1988).

Kennison, Claude. *Colored News of Tallahassee: A Walk Through Time 1855–1995*. Tallahassee: The John G. Riley Center/Museum of African American History & Culture, 1996.

Lewis, Terry E. "Frenchtown: A Geographic Survey of an All-Negro Business District in Tallahassee." MA thesis, Florida State University, 1966.

Menzel, Marjorie. "Frenchtown's Renaissance." *Tallahassee Magazine* 27, no. 4, July–August 2005, 3–8, 10, 12.

Mormino, Gary R. "G.I. Joe Meets Jim Crow: Racial Violence and Reform in World War II." *The Florida Historical Quarterly* 73, no. 1 (July 1994).

Ortiz, Paul. *Emancipation Betrayed—The Hidden History of Black Organizing and White Violence in Florida from Reconstruction to the Bloody Election of 1920*. Berkeley: University of California Press, 2005.

Paisley, Clifton. *The Red Hills of Florida 1528–1865*. Tuscaloosa: University of Alabama Press, 1989.

"Reconstruction: The Second Civil War." *The American Experience*. WGBH Educational Foundation, 1997. http://www.pbs.org/wgbh/amex/reconstruction/program/index.html

Rhodes, Barbara. *At First: The Presbyterian Church In Tallahassee, Florida, 1828–1938.* Tallahassee: First Presbyterian Church, 1994.

Richardson, Joe M. "The Freedmen's Bureau and Negro Labor in Florida." *The Florida Historical Quarterly* 39, no. 2 (October 1960).

"The Ride To Equality: Fifty years after the Tallahassee bus boycott." *Tallahassee Democrat.* Special Report Feature, May 21, 2006. http://www.tallahassee.com

Smith, Charles U. *The Civil Rights Movement In Florida and the United States.* Tallahassee: Father and Son Publications, 1989.

Thompson, Sharyn M.E., and Darlene P. Bowers. *Historical and Architectural Survey of the Frenchtown Neighborhood Tallahassee, Florida, Vol. 1, Final Report.* Tallahassee: The Historic Preservation Board of Trustees, Florida Department of State, Spring 1987.

Vignoles, Charles, civil and topographical engineer. *Observations Upon The Floridas.* 1823. A facsimile reproduction of the first edition with an introduction and index by John Herron Moore. Gainesville: The University Presses of Florida, 1977.

Wilkes, Clayton R. "An Analytic Study of a Tallahassee Slum Section." MA thesis, Florida State University, 1949.

Williams, John Lee. *The Territory of Florida, or sketches of the topography, civil and natural History of the country, the climate, and the Indian tribes from the first discovery to the present time.* 1837. A facsimile reproduction of the first edition. Gainesville: University of Florida, 1962.

Yates, Linda H. *Trinity United Methodist Church: Tallahassee's First Church 1824–1999.* Tallahassee: Trinity United Methodist Church, 1999.

INDEX

INDEX

Trinity Methodist Church 39
Triumph Sanctified Holiness Church 96
Tuskegee Airmen 74

U

Urban League 114

W

Wallace, John 66
Walls, Josiah T. 66
Wells, Nancy 26
West Florida Seminary 44, 50
white primaries 68
Williams, Robert 29

Y

Yellowhair, Maggie 93
yellow fever epidemic 39